HELEN PENFOLD

Remember Cambodia

OMF BOOKS

First published October 1979

ISBN 0 85363 129 8

Made in Great Britain
Published by Overseas Missionary Fellowship,
Belmont, The Vine, SEVENOAKS, Kent, TN13 3TZ
and printed by A. Wheaton & Co. Ltd, Exeter

Contents

Foreword by Michael Griffiths   5
Author's Preface   9
Introduction   11
  1 An Open Door   13
  2 Going In   17
  3 The Silent Years   27
  4 The Call to the Khmers   33
  5 The Rising Tide   42
  6 The Spreading Flame   50
  7 Burning   60
  8 Death Trap   67
  9 Circle of Crisis   73
 10 Hunger for Life   79
 11 Going Out   89
 12 Border Road   99
 13 No Way Back   108
 14 Through the Darkness   115
 15 The Living Stones   126

Foreword

This book is needed to focus Christian attention and prayer upon Cambodia, its people and particularly its Christians. Other books have described what happened in Cambodia when the Khmer Rouge took over, but without any mention either of God or the Christian Church. Helen Penfold's passionate concern for the people of Cambodia shines throughout this book, and that is why it needs to be read.

The reader may be irritated by some imperfections: it is hard to keep a sense of chronology, but that is a product of war, chaos and Cambodia in its agony and thus gives us a realistic picture, for information does not arrive neatly in chronological order. Some discerning readers may also be puzzled by the writer's failure to ask critical questions about some of the events described. But without direct first-hand experience of the missionary situation, she is perhaps wise to relate only what others from Cambodia have reported, without comment. We are therefore grateful to have this book made available, in order to repair our ignorance of the Cambodian scene.

The first question that screams to be asked is how it came about that a country of six million people could have been so long ignored by the Christian world. Even the Christian and Missionary Alliance, with its great work in Vietnam, did not enter Cambodia till 1923, yet there are more Cambodians than Scots or Swiss, and twice as many as there are New Zealanders. The Christian world at large does not seem to notice needy countries until they are brought forcefully to its attention by natural disasters, the tragedy of revolution and war. Even then, they are often quickly forgotten again.

The second question we must ask is about missionary policy in helping to build and establish the Christian church. The Cambodian church had roughly 300 members at the time when the Sihanouk regime fell. Such a small church did not have many gifted, mighty and wise members. Was it in the best interests of the tiny church as a whole to syphon off one leader to distribute Bibles, two for Christian relief, others for radio and student work and so on? That the church needed to apply itself to such interests, and that outside help was both needed and appreciated, is not in question. But do interdenominational societies help a national church by intruding their own organizational structures into such pioneer situations?

We must also ask, how justified were foreign missionaries in splitting a unified national church on a basis of theological controversy from the western world? The tragedy is the lack of thought. It never seems to occur to many people that they might work with the existing church. Short-sighted members at home, because they have not been challenged to think about it, may wish to see a replica of their own denominational structure established abroad. They do not consider that verses like, 'he who destroys the temple of God, him will God destroy' (I Cor. 3.17) might fairly be applied to their own sectarian view of the church.

Thirdly, the book makes us marvel at the patience and providence of God. We meet the almost bizarre appearance of imported singing groups and a view of evangelism that takes no notice of cross-cultural differences in the way the Gospel is expressed. Training courses can be arranged by groups that have no knowledge either of language or of cultural preconceptions about God and the world. But why complain? Nobody else was doing anything at all. At least these people went into a country at war and showed Christian love and concern. And God in His mercy chose to bless it in spite of everything.

Fourthly, the book reveals the agony of missionary

6

withdrawal. The OMF decided that when embassies and consulates ordered the evacuation of their nationals, our missionaries must leave at the same time to avoid any comparisons or complaints. But to leave when national Christians are left behind, weeping at your departure, is unforgettably traumatic. There is agony in knowing that the 'unfinished task' is not a mere cliché of missionary meetings but a desperate reality. Even after the Khmer Church had exploded from three hundred to three thousand in two years, and two Phnom Penh congregations swollen to 27, there was still only one Christian in every two thousand people. If only we had woken up to the need and the opportunity earlier. If only more young people in Europe and America had responded to that need.

This book should make us pray for Cambodia, and especially for refugees from Cambodia, Laos and Vietnam who may be settling in our country now. We must express practical help, not merely with money which can be an abdication of responsibility, but with the costly love that cares for these people for whom Christ died. May we all come to share the passionate concern for Cambodia that Helen Penfold has, and not for Cambodians only but for the whole world.

Michael Griffiths
General Director, Overseas Missionary Fellowship

Author's Preface

I am deeply indebted to many in the writing of this book; the information I have been sent from all over the world has helped me to see much more clearly the Lord's purposes for Cambodia. Chhirc Taing must be mentioned first, with Bophana his wife, because their friendship enriched our lives; Bophana was glad to help me in the writing, although it must have brought her painful memories.

The Christian and Missionary Alliance have done tremendous work for the Cambodian people. Arthur and Esther Hammond, the first evangelical missionaries, sent me a great deal of material, and I want to thank them for the clearest start I could have had to the history of the Church. Eugene Hall sent me a vast amount of material from his own diary of the years 1970 and 1975 about the Cambodian Evangelical Church. Grady Mangham and Andrew Bishop too gave valuable help. Dean and Esther Kroh and I got to know each other through the tapes we exchanged, and I would also like to thank them and other C&MA missionaries.

Tim and Barbara Friberg, of Wycliffe Bible Translators, helped to give me a wider picture of Cambodia, and thanks go to them for all their help. Stanley Mooneyham of World Vision also sent information, and Pene Key and her family helped too. DeAnn and Todd Burke have been a great encouragement, and I have valued their prayers for the book. The tape of Nou Thay was also an inspiration to me.

To the people of OMF I express my warmest thanks — especially to Alice Compain for her suggestions and to Don Cormack, who encouraged me to write this account. My special thanks to Andrew Way, whose friendship and kind suggestions helped me to persevere, and for information past and present. I also want to thank Edyth Banks for her ideas and assistance.

Thanks also to Pauline Giles, who typed the manuscript, and to Tim Lenton, who undertook the necessary rewriting.

My husband Paul had much to put up with, and has given his time to reading the book and suggesting changes. He has also needed the patience of a saint when looking for an ironed shirt! Throughout the writing of this book the Lord has guided, and somehow everything has fallen into place.

Helen Penfold

Cambodia for Christ began in 1973 to raise up prayer and aid for the people of Cambodia. Our aims are to bring to Christians the needs of this land and people wherever they are. Their agony has become our burden.

In 1978 *South East Asian Outreach* was formed. This is an extension of *Cambodia for Christ* aiming to do a similar thing for the peoples of Vietnam and Laos. The suffering of the boat people and other refugees has led us into the vital work of helping people all over the world from these lands. Now we are involved personally in resettling refugees and in other practical ministries; but it all began with prayer.

The Christians in these lands of Cambodia, Laos and Vietnam are undergoing suffering and persecution still, and therefore we need you to join with us to pray and help. Please contact us at:

Cambodia for Christ/South East Asian Outreach
19 Edale Moor,
Liden, SWINDON, Wilts.

Introduction

This book came into being as a result of repeated requests to *Cambodia for Christ* for more information on the Church of Cambodia. Even before the descent of the Bamboo Curtain, there was little available in written form about this unique Church.

The book's aims are to show the impact of the Gospel on Cambodia and its people, and how in the most adverse circumstances the message of God's love can bring healing, hope and new life. It goes without saying that it is a book aimed at stimulating prayer for those at present sitting under the shadow of darkness within Cambodia and those scattered throughout the world. We know only part of the trials, tribulations and persecutions of the Cambodian Church — and their faithfulness — but our responsibility to pray for the believers remains.

Since this book was written, Cambodia has once more experienced radical upheaval. The country is in the care of a Vietnamese-backed Cambodian Communist regime. Nobody knows what that will mean to the people's lifestyle in that small land.

The new regime appears to be encouraging a return to family life and marriages are now allowed freely. However, the future remains uncertain for the numerous refugees throughout the world. The question constantly recurring in their minds is, 'What has happened to my relatives, and will I be able to contact them?'

The agony of waiting with no news remains as some fighting continues, and communication with non-communist countries is limited. From Vietnam letters come out, but as yet this is not true of Cambodia. Our pressing need is to pray. The cruelty of the Khmer Rouge led many to wish for a change in government. Now a new regime is in power there is hope.

The second fall of Phnom Penh is completed, but as yet it is uncertain how this will affect the Christian Church of Cambodia. But we do know one thing—it remains alive!

My own prayer is that this book will help its readers to remember these Cambodians and be encouraged by the faith that so many have demonstrated. The Church of Cambodia may be hidden to us for years, but we can be sure that we will meet its members one day.

1 An Open Door

In 1973 Cambodia was ravaged by war. Chhirc Taing, a Cambodian Christian, was in Britain—but his main aim was to return to his own country.

I met him at a missionary conference in Scotland. He was small, but filled with energy, and he spoke with authority. His deep concern for the beautiful land of Cambodia was very evident, and my husband and I felt the urgency of his call to prayer and action on behalf of the young, dynamic Church there, which was suffering the effects of war and deprivation.

As we got to know Chhirc and his family better, we saw how we could help, and at Chhirc's suggestion *Cambodia for Christ* was born. It began as a letter to people whom Chhirc had met in Britain, to encourage prayer for the Cambodian people. Later it expanded to help the small, growing Church in other ways.

Cambodia had at one time been part of French Indo-China. It is a tropical country and a tourist's paradise: huge temples and ruins dominated the countryside in many places.

Once a huge empire of 30 million people, it was much grander at its peak in the 12th century AD than anything Europe had to offer. But that had long since vanished, and the country's boundaries were greatly reduced. When Chhirc was born, in the busy town of Kompong Cham, the population of Cambodia was about seven million.

Chhirc was the third son of a Christian family of seven brothers and three sisters. His father worked as a motor mechanic, and Chhirc and his brothers received good schooling. As a child Chhirc was very shy, and used to run

13

and hide when visitors came to the house. After leaving school he joined the army; he also became a committed Christian.

At 23 he fell in love with a girl who had recently arrived in Kompong Cham — Bophana, the tenth child of a family of wealthy Christians. Chhirc was friendly with one of her brothers, and with his assistance the couple got together, eventually married, and moved to the capital, Phnom Penh.

Phnom Penh was a modern, bustling city with broad boulevards — a centre of commerce and industry, its own airport linking it easily with the outside world. Good roads and the Mekong river provided transport routes to other parts of Cambodia and South-East Asia.

In Cambodia there are two seasons: dry and wet. Legend relates that six centuries ago, during the rainy season, flood waters washed up a huge Koki tree on the hillside home of a lady named Penh, and when she looked inside the hollow of the trunk she found four bronze Buddhas. To celebrate she built a shrine on the hill, and this became known as the *Wat Phnom*, or Hill Temple. Around this temple the city of Phnom Penh was formed.

Cambodia was a staunchly Buddhist country, and Christians like Chhirc had a very difficult time, particularly if they were well known. During the 1960s Prince Sihanouk, a flamboyant, wealthy and nationalistic character, was Head of State. The Buddhist religious leaders had an enthusiastic supporter in their Prince, who had spent time in a Buddhist monastery. There were about 3,000 monasteries in the country, and more than 20,000 monks dispersed throughout the land; so it was quite common to see saffron-robed monks going from house to house with their begging bowls. Contributions of rice or other things gained 'merit' and helped the giver in his search for enlightenment, or Nirvana.

The monks themselves were the philosophers or thinkers of the community, teaching not only in temples but also in schools. Before pursuing any policy Prince Sihanouk sought their advice, but like most Cambodians he followed other religious practices too; when dealing with foreign affairs he valued particularly the counsel of a certain spirit medium, who was said to contact for him the spirit of a long-dead princess.

In foreign affairs Prince Sihanouk tried to walk the tightrope of neutrality. He was deeply concerned about the possibility of a united Vietnam, and the threat this would present to Cambodian territory. He wanted at first to have relations with both the West and the Communist bloc, including China, and he pursued some socialist policies. But he veered gradually towards the Communists, despite the suspicions of others as to their motives in helping Cambodia.

In 1963 he broke off diplomatic relations with America, and missionaries were forced to leave because of anti-American feeling. In July 1965 the Cambodian Evangelical Church leaders were ordered to close their churches. The Evangelical Church had never been recognised by the Sihanouk government, although the Christian and Missionary Alliance, its founders, had received a measure of recognition.

The small Christian community in Cambodia had about 700 members and seven trained pastors. Three pastors fell away when the churches closed, and the remaining four Christian leaders were imprisoned for refusing to sign a pledge not to preach. Chhirc was among those who remained firmly committed in the face of this persecution, but many others stopped going to Christian meetings, which continued to be held secretly for a while.

In 1970, however, the tide turned, the Sihanouk government was overthrown and his cousin Prince Matak and Marshal Lon Nol came to power. Freedom of religion was declared, and the Church of Cambodia came out into the open again.

Prince Sihanouk went to live in Peking, supporting the Khmer Rouge (Red Cambodians) in his efforts to regain power. The Communist forces started to gain more and more territory, and many fled from their villages as the Khmer Rouge advanced. Bombing in agricultural areas increased, resulting in a flow of refugees—40,000 orphans in 1970 alone—to the shelter of the towns and the cities.

In Phnom Penh there were riots against the Vietnamese, who were feared to be in league with the Viet Cong and aiding and abetting the Khmer Rouge. The Roman Catholic community was depleted rapidly, as thousands of Vietnamese left the country. The one Vietnamese evangelical church, Bethel, ceased to function because of lack of numbers, and it became a Cambodian church.

The new government held a ceremony of allegiance to the State in the Buddhist temple. Chhirc asked to be excused from participating in the Buddhist rites, as it was against his Christian principles. Permission was granted.

In 1971 he became treasurer of the Cambodian Evangelical Church, and soon afterwards he was sent by the government on a course in Britain. He began reading for a postgraduate degree in engineering at Heriot Watt University in Edinburgh, where he was joined later by Bophana. Within a year their long-awaited first child, Janet, was born, but their joy was tempered by sorrow as they read worrying letters from Cambodia.

The high optimism of 1970, when cheering soldiers had left Phnom Penh on their way to battle, waving the handkerchiefs given to them as lucky charms, had faltered and died as the war brought constant stories of human misery and death. A Communist takeover was widely predicted, and the Cambodian Evangelical Church urged Chhirc to return and help them reach people with the Gospel of Christ while there was still time.

Chhirc felt the burden of his own land heavy on his heart during those months of 1973. He felt restless as he compared Britain's churches with those in Cambodia, and he knew he had to return. His wife Bophana decided to stay in Britain with the new baby and follow him later; so he went back alone.

2 Going In

Traders brought Roman Catholicism to Cambodia in exactly the same way that earlier religions had arrived. Most people followed the teaching of Theravada Buddhism*; 15 Buddhist festivals have been recorded, covering all aspects of life from birth to death. Some bear traces of Hindu rites, others of animism. Royalty and peasants alike were captivated by the teaching which for centuries controlled their family life and the nation's strategy. Buddha, the 'Enlightened One', had trapped the inhabitants of Cambodia in a darkness which seemed impenetrable.

The Portuguese traders came in 1553, and several present-day Roman Catholic families are the result of their influence. But it was not a popular religion, partly because of rivalry between Spanish and Portuguese settlers. Father Louis Chevreul, a French missionary visiting the southern part of Cambodia and Phnom Penh, became so disheartened by these conflicts and by Cambodian indifference to his message that in 1665 he left the country. A hundred years later French missionaries returned to find that Roman Catholicism had been established by Spanish Franciscans in 1719, ministering to the Spanish community in Cambodia.

The Vietnamese living in Cambodia had been much more responsive than the Cambodians and there were soon converts and churches in their communities. The Chinese, too, showed interest. A Cambodian Buddhist priest was

---

*The form of Buddhism prevalent in Sri Lanka, Burma, Thailand, Cambodia and Laos. It tends towards a conservative, orthodox interpretation of the Buddha's teaching.

converted after the arrival of the French missionaries, but most Cambodians remained unimpressed by the religion brought by intolerant Westerners.

There were also animistic tribal groups in Cambodia. Known generally as the Khmer Loeu — Upper Khmers — they lived in the mountain regions. One group was situated close to the ancient ruins of Angkor Wat. The hill tribes had been used as slaves in the ancient Cambodian Empire, and even in modern Cambodia they were regarded as inferior; many had little contact with civilisation. The Cham people, a separate ethnic group who intermarried with Cambodian royalty at one time, numbered about 80,000 (1½ per cent of the population), and were Muslim in religion.

Cambodia had become a French protectorate in 1863, and many of its officials were practising Roman Catholics. Since 1770 a Catechism in Cambodian had been available, but no attempt had been made to translate the Bible.

*   *   *

In the early part of the twentieth century Christians on the other side of the world were taking an interest in the obscure country of Cambodia. Two old ladies in America began to pray for its need of the Gospel. In another area a cowboy prayed daily for many years for the Cambodian people.

'One morning,' he wrote, 'while I was interceding for Cambodia, I suddenly felt that there was someone else in the room with me. I couldn't understand it, for there was never anyone in the house but my mother, and she would never interrupt me while I was praying. So I simply stopped praying and quietly worshipped God. After a while a voice spoke to me and told me to stop praying for the opening of Cambodia, and to start praying for the missionaries, for they were there already.'

The same cowboy went on a business trip a few weeks later to Omaha, and visited the Gospel Tabernacle there to hear a famous preacher. To his surprise he felt the urge to ask the preacher if he knew the names of the missionaries in Cambodia — and was told them immediately. So for many years he wrote to them and encouraged them as they faced obstacles and trials in preaching the Gospel.

*   *   *

Arthur Hammond, a young American, went to Bible school at Nyack, the Christian and Missionary Alliance training college, with no thought of the needs of Cambodia. Years beforehand he had said in giving his life to the Lord for overseas service: 'Any place, Lord, but please don't send me to China!' But when he heard a talk by Dr Jaffray, a great C&MA pioneer, he changed his prayer. 'OK, Lord, no strings attached.'

During his second year at Bible college he was given a pamphlet entitled *Cambodia*. He read it and shared the information with his fiancée, Esther. 'It was grim and daunting news', he said, 'for the Buddhist government was hostile to any attempt to proclaim the Gospel.'

Despite the unhopeful outlook the couple committed themselves to serving the Lord in Cambodia, and in 1921 Arthur set sail for Indo-China. It was an unpleasant journey. The ancient coastal steamer was carrying crates of strong-smelling cabbages, and the ship rocked with a deadly motion beneath his feet. During the trip he contracted malaria, and he arrived exhausted in Saigon to begin language study. There he found he was expected to live day and night on a mission compound learning Vietnamese, and the other missionaries discouraged him from going to Cambodia. 'We are short enough of workers here', they said.

Arthur did not argue, but prayed about his burden for Cambodia. At the annual conference he spoke with Dr Jaffray once more about the country, and Dr Jaffray preached to the whole conference on the need for sacrifices — and a pioneering spirit. 'The Vietnamese field was won by many personal sacrifices, and there are three and a-half million souls in Cambodia waiting to hear the message of Jesus Christ', he said. After this there was no more talk of Arthur remaining in Vietnam!

Not long afterwards a senior missionary went as a tourist to Cambodia and tried to contact an official about starting missionary work there. The reply received was abrupt and to the point: 'Cambodia has no place for Christian missionaries.'

The door to Cambodia seemed slammed shut; so Arthur turned his thoughts to the 90,000 Cambodians living in the Travinh region of Vietnam. 'At least that way', he reasoned, 'I can learn the Cambodian language.' Mr Irwin, a senior missionary, made arrangements to take him and introduce him to officials of the province. But on the day they were to make the trip Mr Irwin had a surprise for Arthur. 'I have been praying about this trip', he said, 'and I believe we should try to get into Cambodia first.'

The unexpected good news made Arthur so elated that he hardly noticed the bumps and rattles that threatened to shake their ramshackle old bus apart on the road to the Cambodian capital. And the next day in Phnom Penh his excitement was even greater. To their astonishment the pair managed to obtain an audience with the official, who proved strangely helpful.

'If you want to preach the Gospel in Cambodia', he said, 'I do not know anything to stop you. You will have no success, but you can try if you like.'

It transpired that this was a new official: the man the first missionary had seen was on extended leave. They decided to act quickly before he returned, and sent immediately for more missionaries. Arthur had to go back to Saigon for his language exams, but Esther came out from America on December 28, 1922, and they were married the next month in Saigon. After a brief honeymoon they moved to Phnom Penh, and found rooms and a language teacher there.

Eight months passed before they were joined by David

and Muriel Ellison, who were sent by the C&MA to the large provincial town of Battambang. David was asked to open a Bible school there, which he did in 1925. It had five students—Cambodians from South Vietnam who had been converted in that country through Cambodian Christian literature. A Thai agent of the British and Foreign Bible Society had persuaded a Cambodian to translate the Gospel of Luke and the Acts of the Apostles, and through reading these pieces of Scripture the five Cambodians had committed their lives to Christ.

Another Cambodian translation of Luke was also available—the result of a French Christian official's concern to reach the people with the Gospel—but the translation of the complete Bible became the responsibility of the Hammonds. It was a very difficult task; people tended to be hostile, and they had no reference books or dictionaries to help them. After long, arduous years the New Testament was printed in Hanoi in 1934, and by 1940 the Old Testament was completed. But then disaster struck: in the same year the government brought out a dictionary which made any previous phonetic system redundant. The Hammonds and the literature committee had no choice but to begin again. The Bible was finally completed and printed by the British and Foreign Bible Society in 1954—31 years after the Hammonds had arrived in Cambodia.

Other obstacles faced the early Protestant missionaries, and progress was difficult in the 1920s. The first, antagonistic official eventually returned from leave and, finding that the Hammonds were living in Phnom Penh and proclaiming the Gospel, he began to harass them. He accused them of anti-government activities and placed restrictions on their movements. When they complained, the Sureté (Secret Police) told them: 'These restrictions are to ensure your safety and are for your benefit.'

Arthur was told to report where they went on their visits, and even the exact times of leaving and returning to their house. 'We were also aware of being followed en route', he said later, 'because men wearing dark glasses and riding bicycles stopped every time we halted.'

As the Hammonds seemed undeterred, the official decided to make things more difficult. One day he called them to his office and said: 'You must only visit places where you have converts—and I want a list of your converts.' Reluctantly, Arthur gave him a list. When they tried to contact the converts again, they were unable to trace them.

Once more the official called them in. 'If you spread your message you will be expelled from Cambodia', he said. And the Secret Police ordered: 'No Cambodians must come to your meetings, and the chapel sign must come down.'

Close to despair, they went home and began to pray. They decided to leave the sign up and ignore prohibitions, because they knew people were praying for them. A week passed, and nothing happened. They became curious, and asked questions. Soon the answer came: 'Didn't you know? The chief of the Sureté has left, because he detests the climate.'

After seven years the Hammonds went on leave, then returned to Battambang, the City of Flowers, to enable the Ellisons to go on furlough. The Bible school students had been out in the countryside over the previous year, sharing their faith, and during that year a Cambodian ferryman, Ta Kruic, became a believer. He was from Kompong Cham, where Chhirc was born, and he became an elder in the church there. Everyone who used Ta Kruic's ferry received a tract.

When Arthur and Esther arrived in Battambang they found a much greater freedom. But it did not last long. One day Arthur spotted the anti-Christian official from Phnom Penh driving past in his car. Later a colporteur was selling Gospels in the street when a car drew up beside him. 'A man jumped out, snatched the Gospel from my hand and tore it up', he told Arthur—and the missionary had no doubts about the identity of the driver.

But a week passed without further incident. Then came the surprising news that another enemy of the Gospel had departed. He too, it seemed, 'couldn't stand the climate'.

The official's leaving, however, did not signal the end of opposition. The Bible school was treated with suspicion by the authorities, and in 1928 it was closed. Then, in December 1932, an edict forbidding the proselytising of Cambodians was published. In Battambang this edict was kept on file, and with some hesitation the authorities allowed the chapel to remain open, but in other regions things were not so easy.

A student preacher in Kratie province was thrown into gaol and afterwards ordered to leave the province, but not before Christian families had been created there and a small church established. A missionary couple working there were transferred, and were not replaced for 18 years. But when the new missionaries arrived in 1950 they found a family from Kbal Chuor who had been praying faithfully over the years for another missionary to come.

In Siem Reap province people were interrogated by the police and threatened. One student preacher was called to see the governor, who told him not to visit a certain family. 'They do not wish to see you or become Christians', he said. The student told David Ellison, who decided to risk a visit. When he arrived at the house the husband said, 'I was told that if we believed we would be imprisoned.' Nevertheless the missionary was welcomed, and the family listened eagerly to what he had to say. That night five more believed.

Because of the anxiety among Cambodian Christians in Siem Reap, David Ellison decided to try a direct approach. He went to the governor and told him, 'the edict does not mean persecuting people.'

Enraged, the governor went to the French authorities, who gave him an unexpected reply: 'Do not interfere unless it is a political matter.' Shortly afterwards the governor was transferred.

In later years there seemed to be no attempt to enforce

the edict, and in 1946 a further edict was issued, ensuring religious liberty. Believers were scattered and isolated, but many had kept faith over the years. Some had met at an annual church conference, but otherwise there was little contact between Christians.

In 1949 the Bible school was transferred to TaKhmau, five miles outside Phnom Penh. The Issarak rebellion — a bid to end French domination of Cambodia — had begun three years previously, and there was general disruption in the countryside. On one trip from Phnom Penh to Battambang David Ellison and a Cambodian helper, Kru Kim Aun, were fired on by a sub-machine gun. A bullet entered the car, passed through David's trousers and just missed his groin, but Kru Kim Aun, a gentle and respected Christian, was severely injured by a bullet which creased his forehead, and was rushed to hospital, where he had a major brain operation. He later recovered and worked as a pastor in Kratie province.

Many Christians came to the annual conference at TaKhmau during the rebellion, and as some were returning to Battambang the train they were in was derailed by a terrific explosion. One Christian fell on his face amidst the Buddhist chantings and called out: 'Lord, protect us.' He then recited the 91st Psalm three times. Many that day were killed or captured by the rebels, but all the Christians were spared.

Kru Bun, a Cambodian with a Christian wife, was called up to fight against the rebels. He vowed, 'If I am spared, Lord, I will give myself to your service.' Later he became a pastor of a church at Kampot, and vice-president of the Cambodian Christian Alliance.

As Christians became more numerous, the need for literature became more pressing. The Gospel Press of Cambodia was set up in Phnom Penh, and by the 1960s it had printed three million pages, including Scriptures, church calendars and books. In 1951 a Cambodian Christian magazine, *Bread of Life*, was founded.

But one section of Cambodia was not being reached by

the message of Christ — the tribal villages. In 1952 many of these villages were in enemy hands and inaccessible. Not to be defeated, but not knowing what the result would be, some Christians used a plane to drop tracts and leaflets on one area. Later a man who had picked up one of these tracts came across some Christians, and said, 'I am far away from the Father and I wish to become a Christian.' After his conversion he returned to his village to tell others of his discovery.

When C&MA missionary Merle Graven became director of the TaKhmau Bible school, the Mnong Beit tribal people came to his notice. Just as he was about to suggest that the students should spend their long vacation contacting these tribal groups, he was interrupted by one of his audience, who said, 'I have been spoken to by the Lord, and he told me to spend my vacation in reaching the tribal people.'

In 1953 Ed Thompson, who was later to lose his life in South Vietnam, stayed one evening in a primitive hut with the headman of a tribal village, who arranged some entertainment for his unexpected guest. Someone began to sing a song about God creating the world. Ed listened intently. The singer sang of man falling into sin and of the coming of the Flood, but then the song came to an abrupt halt. Ed asked the singer to carry on, but the headman told him: 'We cannot go on. We don't know any more.' Ed told him: 'I can finish the story for you.'

They all listened eagerly as he explained how Jesus Christ came into the world to save men. When he had finished, the headman asked him to repeat the story. He did so, and when he had finished a second time, there was a long pause. Then the headman said, 'We believe what you tell us is true, but before we believe and pray, can you come here and be our teacher? For if we pray and then return to our heathen ways, the judgement upon us will be twice as great.'

Ed tried to get government permission to live in the area, but he was refused. It would be some years before that village was contacted again.

There was much work to do and too few doing it, and yet despite all the setbacks a small Church was growing. The seed had been planted by prayer, and the future was in the hands of the Lord.

3 The Silent Years

It was not surprising, in a small country fighting so often to preserve its territorial boundaries, that any Cambodian who did not follow the traditional social patterns should become a target for criticism. If a Cambodian associated with foreigners and their foreign religion, it suggested to many that he might be an enemy agent, and therefore a traitor. A change of religion was not just a matter for the individual; it had serious social implications, as Christians like Lim Chheong discovered.

Lim Chheong (known in Chinese as San Hay Seng) was a boy of ten when he first went to a missionary's house. 'I had no real interest in Christianity, but was attracted to the meetings because they used old Christmas cards as prizes', he said. He was a member of a large family but was not interested in the traditional Buddhism, having rejected all religion after his cousin had died in spite of a ceremony to appease evil spirits. He was deeply disillusioned, but Bible stories of a God who cared and would always be with him impressed him so much that in 1948 he became a Christian.

His mother noticed at once that her eldest son had changed, and was dismayed when she found what had happened. His father, who was a silversmith—making idols and objects of worship—reacted more violently. 'I order you to stop believing in this Jesus!' he shouted.

'That I cannot do', replied Lim Chheong. 'I have become a follower of the true God, and I cannot follow the Buddhist way any longer.'

The father became more and more incensed at his son's

stubbornness. One night he even shut him out of the house, telling him to 'go sleep with Jesus.' But Lim Chheong persisted in his belief, and his father decided in the end that he would have to die. 'I have ten children', he thought. 'It is better that I have nine than to have one following the foreigners' religion.'

So he hired a man to kill his son, but on the critical night Lim Chheong returned home a different way, and the plot was foiled — then abandoned.

When Lim Chheong was older and had been on Bible courses he felt that God wanted him to become a pastor. He had just been offered a government course in meteorology, which had pleased his parents; so he was uncertain what to do. His doubts were resolved when he was struck down by a serious illness. Suddenly everything seemed clear. 'Christ was the only person who could bring any meaning to life', he said.

He set off for TaKhmau Bible school disowned by his father, and with his mother weeping bitterly as he left the house. He had nothing — not even the money to get to TaKhmau. Some Christians paid his fare. During his four years at Bible school he lived hand to mouth, but never went hungry.

In his last year at TaKhmau Lim Chheong heard that his mother was seriously ill in hospital, and he went to see her. During the visit, only a few months before her death, his mother placed her trust in Christ.

In 1964, after a period of study in the Philippines, this talented and dedicated man who had come through difficult years took over from Merle Graven as director of TaKhmau Bible school.

*   *   *

Son Sonne studied in a Buddhist temple in South Vietnam between the ages of eight and 16, seeking the meaning of life and fulfilment in Nirvana. His uncle, the abbot of the temple, showed commendable understanding of his nephew's character. 'It isn't necessary to be a monk to find fulfilment', he told him. 'Even in the world outside you can find the way.'

Eventually Son Sonne left the monastery and went to Phnom Penh, seeking a new life, reality and truth. Somehow a copy of the book of Proverbs came into his hands. 'I was struck with the profound wisdom it contained, and it led me to seek more of God', he said.

His search for meaning was bearing fruit, but he was troubled by the concepts of sin and heaven, and remained dissatisfied until he went with his fiancée to the Cambodian Evangelical Church. On Christmas Day 1962, at the age of 24, he committed his life to Christ. His fiancée made the same decision, and a few months later they were married.

It was not long before eagerness to tell his workmates about his faith led to his being sacked from his job for 'giving out all this literature'. But it soon became clear that he and his wife should go to TaKhmau Bible school. They began a course there in 1963, and Son Sonne soon became known as a smiling, vibrant preacher.

*   *   *

As a teenager in high school, Yos Oan took up repairing old radios as a hobby. One day, as he was tuning in to another frequency, he chanced on a Far East Broadcasting Company (FEBC) programme. Someone was speaking about a man called Jesus Christ, and Yos Oan was interested enough to listen intently, because he had never heard of him before. At the end of the programme an address was given, and he wrote to it at once. A few days later he received some tracts, which he read avidly. He then went around discussing their contents; he even went to the Buddhist temple and talked about it with the monks. Later he went to look for the Cambodian Church; one Sunday he arrived at Bethany Church in Phnom Penh and dedicated his life to Christ.

Not much later Yos Oan found himself in prison for his

faith. He, Son Sonne, Lim Chheong and another Christian were the four arrested in July 1965, when the president of the National Church was ordered to close all the churches, and they were asked to sign a pledge not to preach about Jesus Christ. All refused.

With four of its leaders in prison, the Christian community was dismayed. Those who remained faithful met nightly to pray for the men's release, and Chhirc Taing went each day to stand at the prison gates 'to show I was still standing for the Lord'. Bophana and the wives of the imprisoned men met each morning at four o'clock to prepare food to take to the prison an hour later. The guards were persuaded to pass it on to the prisoners.

Chhirc Taing even went to the police and complained. 'Why have you imprisoned these men?' he asked. 'They are not spies. They are loyal to our country.'

It was probably only the mutual suspicion of police and army that saved Chhirc from arrest. He was accused of being sympathetic to foreigners and threatened with the loss of his job. But he retorted: 'I do not follow the Americans. I follow Jesus Christ.' And he persisted with his demands that the prisoners should be released. His daily visits to the police brought a warning to his wife, but even this did not deter him. He visited the prisoners too — and never did lose his job. After three months, the four were released.

At about the same time the building where the Christians had met was stoned, and Christians were shouted at in the street. Others were questioned and threatened, among them a pastor from Kampot named Nou Thay.

Nou Thay had been born into a Christian home, and as a small child he had fallen sick and died. A small coffin was made for his body, but his grief-stricken mother raised his body up before the Lord and said: 'Lord, if you will raise this son of mine, I will let him serve you when he grows up.' At that moment Nou Thay opened his eyes and asked for something to eat.

At the age of 17 Nou Thay was strong and robust. He

consecrated his life to Christ after a meeting which, he noted, 'sent everybody else to sleep'.

Nou Thay felt that he should go to Bible school, but he could not afford it. His prayers were answered when a missionary handed him some money sent for 'a promising student'. It came from the parents of an American girl who had been saving it to go to Bible school herself—but had died. Nou Thay was amazed that he should be given the money, because he had not spoken about his desire to go to Bible school. He set off immediately for TaKhmau.

Nou Thay went to work in Kampot when the missionaries left in 1965. Shortly afterwards he was called in to face the local governor, who smiled kindly at him. 'Nou Thay, how glad I am to see you', he said. 'Of course, now that the Americans have left you have no support. You will have to make a living teaching English.'

'I have come to Kampot to carry on the work of the Lord, whether there are Americans or not', said Nou Thay.

The governor paused, still smiling. 'Well, what if you get arrested?'

Nou Thay, without hesitating, responded: 'I have surrendered my life to Christ, and if necessary I am willing to go to jail for Christ's sake.'

Angry, the governor shouted: 'If that's the way you feel, you can get out!'

Relieved, Nou Thay returned to his work.

Though no American missionaries remained after 1965, there were two French missionary couples in Cambodia—the Funés and the Clavauds. Jean and Roselyne Clavaud had been with the C&MA in the early 60s, but were now working independently with the Cambodian Evangelical Church. Jean taught part-time, and Roselyne ran a small kindergarten. In Siem Reap Jean worked with a Cambodian pastor named Chau Uth, who had once been a farmer. A small, wiry man whose devotion to the Lord was greatly admired (he would later become president of the Cambodian Church), Chau Uth visited the small villages and pagodas with Jean. Everyone listened, but there was little obvious response.

In 1965 they moved to Phnom Penh, where the Clavauds did their best to help Chau Uth and his eight children, whose financial support from C&MA had been cut off when the Americans were forced to leave.

When the four Christian leaders were released from jail, the Christians rejoiced. Lim Chheong had led 12 people to the Lord while he was in prison, and so the Church was growing in spite of persecution. Son Sonne, on his release, moved with his family to a former youth centre, where a small fellowship gathered, and from this group two other churches sprang in 1971.

During the unsettled years of 1965 to 1970 a small, strong Cambodian Church grew up. But Cambodia's problems were only beginning. In 1970 a visitor to the country stood watching young people march past him in a special ceremony to mark a new government. 'Their faces made a distinct impression on me', he wrote. 'Then the Holy Spirit spoke to me, saying: "This one is going to die, and that one, and that one." '

The need to pray for Cambodia remained with him as he left that country. And his prayers were badly needed, because the war was already bringing with it a harvest of suffering, deprivation and death which was to touch the lives of all the Cambodian people.

4 The Call to the Khmers

The airport was almost deserted as the plane landed at Phnom Penh and two passengers emerged. The sun shone brilliantly on the beautiful city, but the sandbagged bunkers and the barbed wire were a sharp reminder that Cambodia was at war. So the waiting official was quite taken aback when one of the passengers told him: 'I am here to stay.'

The man was Gene Hall, and he and his wife Carol were one of three American C&MA couples invited by the Cambodian Evangelical Church to return to Cambodia early in 1970. Merle Graven, the C&MA director, and his wife and Norman and Marie Ens were the others. They were only too anxious to accept the invitation.

The Cambodian Christians had not been inactive in the five-year interval. The first one Gene met was a pastor on his way back to Takeo to rebuild a church which had been destroyed by the Viet Cong. In the street, Gene was handed a tract by an old Chinese elder, practically blind, who went around the boulevards of Phnom Penh distributing tracts at the rate of 2,000 a week.

In the chaos of war the Church of Cambodia was free to worship and witness, and the Christians were using their opportunities. There was also a new sense of unity; their prayer was: 'Lord, show us how we can reach Cambodia for Christ.' Prayer cells started meeting throughout the city two or three times a week after Gene and three Cambodians—Son Sonne, Lim Chheong and Minh Thien Voan—had been filled with a tremendous burden for the Cambodian people while standing together in an open field.

Minh Thien Voan was a stocky, fair-skinned, very zealous man who had become a Christian while on a course in America. His Cambodian boss, whom many disliked and feared because of his strong temper, described him as a man of patience, endurance and honesty in whom he had absolute trust.

The war brought destruction of life, and as usual the innocent were the victims. The Christians were concerned as they saw the cycle of carnage and senseless brutality which was fast making Cambodia a nation of refugees. In July 1970 the Cambodian Church leaders were told informally that the government would welcome any help they could give refugees—and they would also be allowed to preach the Gospel.

The supply routes to Phnom Penh were being attacked, and so personal hardship was encountered by the poorer people. Vietnam's war was now Cambodia's problem, and at night the darkness was haunted by the sound of machine-gun fire.

At about this time World Vision, a large Christian relief organisation, had become interested in Cambodia. Its director, Dr Stanley Mooneyham, had been uncertain whether to become involved with Cambodia as well as South Vietnam, and had prayed for guidance. As he did so the words of Ecclesiastes 2 came into his mind: 'If you wait for perfect conditions you will never get anything done.'

It was a hazardous journey to Phnom Penh in February 1970. People told him: 'You are wrong to go. You are risking the lives of all who go with you.' But Dr Mooneyham was used to making hard decisions, and he thought first of the people of Cambodia. The road was mined and often attacked by the Khmer Rouge, yet miraculously the convoy of lorries arrived safely in Phnom Penh, carrying their supplies of medical drugs and equipment.

In July 1970 he made the journey again and offered to help the Cambodian Church in its refugee outreach. Son Sonne had begun teaching English in a school, and half of his wages were used for evangelism. There were 60,000 refugees in the city, and much to be done.

*   *   *

The risks that the World Vision team took earned for Christians generally the respect of the staunch Buddhist government. Two Cambodian government officials were on a visit to Saigon when they stopped outside the headquarters of SIL — Wycliffe Bible Translators' Summer Institute of Linguistics. They were seen gazing at the sign by Tim Friberg, the business manager, and his wife Barbara, who were learning Vietnamese and hoping to work later with the Cham tribespeople in Vietnam.

Tim had been too busy to go to the annual SIL conference in Nha Trang in January 1971, and found the two Cambodians outside his HQ when he arrived one day. He asked them where they came from, and one replied: 'We have learnt of your translation work, and have come to meet you. We are on a course of education in Saigon and come from Cambodia.'

Tim invited them in and told them about the work of the Wycliffe Bible Translators, who had been in Vietnam for 15 years.

'Why have you never been to Cambodia?' they asked, amazed.

He replied: 'I don't know. I guess it was because we were never invited.'

He was quickly given an invitation to work in Cambodia, and phoned Nha Trang to pass on the news. The Fribergs were still not sure whether to work among the Cham people in Vietnam or Cambodia, but a visit to Cambodia and the city of Phnom Penh made up their minds. 'We were impressed by everything we saw, and felt that this was the place we should be.'

They moved to Phnom Penh in February 1972 and lived with a Cambodian family, studying the language, for three months. In May they moved into their own home, and on

July 4th began preparing Cham reading primers. Their work among the Cambodian Cham had begun.

*   *   *

Among the 450,000 Chinese in Cambodia there were churches in Phnom Penh and Battambang which had some links with the C&MA. These were pastored by Chinese missionaries, one of whom was Samuel Mok. As a talented young man in China he had come to the notice of the Communists, who wanted him to work for them. But he refused. 'I can't do that', he said, 'as I believe in God and you do not. In any case, God has called me to be a preacher.'

When they saw they were getting nowhere, they threatened him by putting a revolver to his heart. 'Join us or we will kill you', they said.

'Go ahead. If you shoot me I'll be with Jesus', said Samuel. 'He lives in my heart.'

At this one of the Communists drew a knife and said: 'We'll cut your heart out and see if he still lives there.'

'All right', said Samuel, 'but you won't see him, because you can't see him with the physical eye. He's spiritual.'

So the Communists dragged him off to prison, where they beat him to try to persuade him to change his mind — without effect. Then they tried starving him, but the other prisoners secretly gave him food. At last the guards came to him and said: 'We will let you go if you promise never to preach on Genesis 1.'

He replied: 'I can never promise that. I must preach the whole Bible.'

But he was eventually released, and went to live in Cambodia in the early 1950s. There he became pastor of the Chinese church in Battambang, where he served with great dedication, turning down offers of big congregations in Hong Kong and Saigon. 'You find me a pastor for my small church here in Battambang, and I will come to your churches', he said — knowing that no volunteers would be forthcoming. He was joined by Miriam Ho and Daniel Lam, and they worked as a team to reach the Chinese in Cambodia.

*   *   *

The Overseas Missionary Fellowship was showing an interest in Cambodia during the 1970s, and in late 1973 overseas director Denis Lane went to prepare a report on the country. He was met by Gene Hall and Chau Uth, now president of the Cambodian Evangelical Church. He stayed four days — and in this short time the opportunities for OMF were obvious. So Denis prayed: 'Lord, if you want OMF to be involved, please lead some Cambodian to yourself when I preach.' At the morning service when he spoke, seven people responded to the message he gave and committed themselves to Christ.

He returned to OMF headquarters in Singapore eager for OMF to help Cambodia. He reported to a council meeting, and what he said was underlined by Chhirc Taing, who happened to be returning from Britain at the time and had stopped off at Singapore. He spoke at a Friday prayer meeting on the needs of Cambodia, and everyone there said they had an acute sense of the Lord's presence. The medical officer quoted a verse that had come to her attention — 'Quit praying, and get the people moving' — and the historic decision to go into Cambodia was taken.

Denis Lane wrote: 'Anyone who goes in must face realistically the danger involved, and be very conscious of the Lord's own commission to Him, for the political future of Cambodia is anything but clear, and the constant thunder of guns and the rattle of tanks as they pass the church prayer meeting do not allow you to forget it.'

*   *   *

Andrew Way was an English missionary working with Thai students in Bangkok when OMF asked him to go to

Cambodia. He was told that there were many needs among students and young people in Phnom Penh.

'As I studied the book of Acts and noted the reasons why St Paul moved on to another place, I saw the call of Macedonia and the needs and urgency of the task', he said. He accepted the Cambodian invitation; his Thai friends afterwards referred to Cambodia as the 'Samaria of Thailand'.

Andrew arrived on March 19th, 1974, and was met at the airport by Chhirc Taing and his cousin, Minh Thien Voan. As Andrew and his Thai friend Sathapon went out on the streets of the city to give out tracts, none was refused. 'Motor cycles drew up at the kerb to look at them, and people crossed the roads to receive one', said Andrew. It was a wonderful experience of the openness of the people of Phnom Penh.

Andrew moved into an eleven-room centre which had been set up jointly by OMF, C&MA and the Cambodian Evangelical Church to reach the young people of Phnom Penh.

*   *   *

There were now several missionary societies working in Cambodia, but not all foreign helpers were affiliated to a society. One such young couple, Todd and DeAnn Burke, from Tulsa, Oklahoma, came to Cambodia in September 1973 after two years of waiting for the way to open.

They had been in Japan, relieving a pastor on holiday, when someone had prophesied: 'God has set before you an open door that no man can shut, and though there are many difficulties, that is the place you should be.' When they arrived, Cambodia's beauty had been marred by the war, and the city of Phnom Penh was crowded with refugees.

Todd and DeAnn worked independently of the Cambodian Evangelical Church, but they were joined by two of their pastors, Kuch Kong and Nou Thay. Kuch

Kong had found them an apartment, and Nou Thay got to know them well. 'As soon as we met, there was an affinity between us, and we believed God sent him to us', said DeAnn. Nou Thay and Todd became very close, as Nou Thay often interpreted when Todd preached. Eventually they formed their own society, known as the Cambodian Charismatic Christian Mission.

*   *   *

A man who came to Cambodia from quite different motives was Jimmy Rim (Rim Se Jong), a karate instructor who had no intention of becoming a Christian, let alone a missionary, when he arrived in 1973. He was a Korean whose mother was a Christian, converted in Seoul, where her family had fled as refugees from North Korea. On the journey south Jimmy, a boy of eight, was separated from them and would have starved if he had not been resourceful. 'I shined shoes, rifled through garbage pails and sifted dirt to get grain that spilled from sacks', he said.

Miraculously, he was found eventually by his elder brother—but he was in for a shock. When he came home he found his family was now a Christian one: three of his brothers and sisters had believed. 'I thought they had wasted their time', he said.

Jimmy became a karate instructor and moved to Saigon, where he trained a unit of Cambodian soldiers. He was later invited to Phnom Penh—to his surprise, as he had a bad reputation. He had violent temper tantrums, when he threw everything in sight. 'Bar owners did not dare ask me to pay the bill', he said. He moved to Phnom Penh marked out as a trouble-maker, and for six months he was just that.

Then in August 1973 he had a nightmare, in which he 'felt petrol was being poured on top of me, and a strange, white-clothed person was standing over me'. He woke up thinking it was an omen of his death by rocket attack. He went out to breakfast at a Korean restaurant, and as he was eating he noticed across the road a building with a cross on top of it. Without knowing why, he went inside.

'I cried and wept for two hours. I had no reason for it, except for the nightmare', he said.

After that he felt ashamed, and wondered if anyone had noticed that a tough black belt karate expert had been crying in church. For the next five days he avoided all contact with people, keeping to his room or visiting the church where he had wept. He tried to smoke, but it gave him a headache. He tried to drink, but it made him feel sick. He was thoroughly miserable. In the end he began to pray.

And he heard a voice—three words, 'Jimmy, give up.' Those three words changed his life. He was the last one in his family to become a Christian. His mother had risen every morning at 4.30 for ten years to pray for his conversion—and at last her faithfulness was rewarded.

Two months later Jimmy heard the voice again: 'Jimmy, I want you to take care of children.' He was puzzled, because he was a single man, but he made his way along to the restaurant and was thinking about it when a dirty, smelly little boy came over to him and said: 'I want to come and stay with you.'

Jimmy pushed him away with his foot, but the little boy came back again. Jimmy said crossly: 'Go home to your parents.'

'I haven't any parents', said the boy.

Jimmy thought about it again. 'All right', he said. 'You can come and live with me.' He took the little boy home and washed, fed and clothed him.

The next day Jimmy went to work as usual, but returned home to find the little boy very unhappy.

'Why are you so unhappy?' he asked.

'I have no friends to play with', said the boy. 'Could I bring another friend to live with us?'

Jimmy agreed, and the boy went off. Later he returned—with *seven* friends.

Jimmy soon received a visit from an obviously frightened

landlord, who begged him to leave. 'I have had many complaints about the boys off the streets who live with you', he said. His relief was overwhelming when the formerly violent Jimmy agreed quietly to look for somewhere else to live.

Jimmy worked hard and eventually 'found a place with all the windows blown out, where I was given a three-year lease. We moved in there and then.' The Cambodian Christians helped to make the place habitable, and the Angel Christian Orphanage was born.

Within three months Jimmy had 100 children to care for. He taught them English and karate, and Korean hymns—he did not know any Cambodian ones. He hired teachers for the children, left his job and began trusting the Lord for his daily needs. Sometimes God provided for them in unusual ways as the children learnt to pray and sing instead of stealing and fighting.

The Buddhist neighbours were openly hostile to the orphanage at first, shouting after Jimmy in the street: 'Take your foreign religion away from here! We don't want you!' But gradually there was a change, and the neighbourhood children began to come along to Jimmy's school, until there were about 300 attending. One of the most antagonistic neighbours even donated a desk and chair.

No one thinks of Jimmy as foreign now. When asked 'What is your nationality?' he replies: 'I am not Korean; I am Cambodian. In Phnom Penh I was born again.'

5 The Rising Tide

Times of crisis often bring the best opportunities, and this was certainly true of the city of Phnom Penh and the country of Cambodia. The war seemed like a sea which constantly advanced and receded, but each time the tide came in, it came in closer. In 1970, for example, Pochentong Airport had been 90 per cent destroyed by shellfire, but the Khmer Rouge were driven back.

But the war in Cambodia saw a unique movement of the Holy Spirit. After 1970 the chance to preach about Christ was always there, simply because everyone wanted to talk about God. To meet the demand for reading material a Christian literature team was set up, with three Cambodians in charge—Sarun, Tauoch and Sonan. On October 21st that year Sonan sold 248 pieces of literature; on December 1st Sarun reported that in ten weeks he had distributed 49,300 tracts.

Back in 1965, after his release from prison, Son Sonne had met a young lawyer named Men Ny Borin. Men Ny Borin had parked his car, come across to where Son Sonne was selling Christian literature and asked what he was doing.

Son Sonne hesitated, then said: 'I am selling literature about Jesus.'

Men Ny Borin smiled. 'Oh, Jesus is wonderful. I have read what Gandhi says about Jesus and become interested in Him. I would like a Bible.'

By 1970 Men Ny Borin had become a judge with a reputation for integrity; Son Sonne and Chhirc Taing decided to pay him a visit and find out how interested he was in Christianity. They were ushered into his office, and the first thing they noticed was an open Bible on his desk. The judge had not been going to church, but he had obviously been reading his Bible! Later he brought his wife and family along to the English school where Son Sonne taught. 'I want my family to become Christians', he said. On October 28th he went to the Bible study group and testified: 'I don't know when I became a Christian, but I do know Jesus Christ as my Saviour now.'

This man later became Judge of the Supreme Court.

Times had certainly changed. The judge who had imprisoned Son Sonne was himself in prison awaiting trial, and Chhirc and Son Sonne visited him. He accepted a tract eagerly, and asked if he could read some others. That was one surprise for the Christians. Another came when a Christian delegation to help refugees was given a chauffeur-driven Mercedes by the government.

But the Cambodian Evangelical Church kept a clear head, and was not seduced by its sudden popularity—as one well-known American Christian leader discovered. He came to Cambodia offering money and promising plenty more, but was told firmly: 'You can keep your money. We don't want it; we just want your prayers.'

Although there was great openness to the Gospel, it was not always accepted gladly. Carol Hall, who had travelled through dangerous country to join her husband Gene, started a Bible study group. One day she was speaking about the evil in a man's heart when one of the Cambodian students slammed the Bible shut angrily.

Then Son Sonne was approached in the street by a lieutenant who asked him: 'Why do you try to force people to believe in God?'

'I don't try to force people to believe', he said. 'I just tell them about Jesus Christ. They must decide for themselves whether it is good or bad teaching.'

But there were few obstacles to the forward march of Christianity in the midst of war. Minh Thien Voan, whose name means Heavenly Messenger, saw his mother become a Christian after a dream in which she saw Christ on the

Cross and heard the words: 'Jesus Christ died to save you.'

A pastor from Kampot, who was later to become a missionary in Vietnam, told a colleague: 'I have lost everything. I have lost my ox, my pigs, my house and furniture. You know I was trying to save some for my children, and now I have lost all.' But he continued: 'I have started with a clear slate, and from now on my life is all for Christ till I meet Him. I am burning all my bridges behind me.'

One day an arrogant Army captain came up to this indomitable old man and started arguing with him about Christianity. In the end the captain said: 'You know, I have never lost an argument before.' The pastor replied: 'I am just an ignorant old farmer. It is Jesus Christ who has won.' The captain became a Christian and was always grateful to his 'ignorant old farmer'.

Some Christians found themselves trapped behind Communist lines because of the rapid advance of enemy forces. On September 19th, 1970, Jean Clavaud and his 12-year-old son Oliver were travelling to Takeo to visit a church there. They were captured and taken under guard to a village nearby, where they were accused of being CIA agents. 'We know what to do with our enemies!' the Communists shouted.

Jean and his son prayed and sang, and although they had no Bible the words of Psalm 50 comforted Jean: 'Call on me in the day of your distress, and I will deliver you and you will glorify me.'

Oliver was allowed some freedom and made friends, but there seemed little hope of escape; although the local peasants felt sorry for them, they were afraid of the Communists. Then on January 3rd, 1971, the impossible happened: they were released through the intervention of one of their captors, who had been a student of Jean's. Many had prayed for their release, and their family were overjoyed when they returned safely to Phnom Penh.

No news had been received for many months about the

Rev Chau Uth, who was behind enemy lines with his wife, and the Christians were anxious for their welfare. There was great relief when they eventually arrived at Phnom Penh and told their story.

They had been travelling with an oxcart on the road towards Phnom Penh when they were stopped and searched by Khmer Rouge soldiers. The soldiers pulled out the contents of the oxcart and prodded everything, asking Chau Uth and his wife where they were going. Chau Uth replied: 'We are going to visit a friend.' Both knew that if the soldiers discovered their Bible their lives could be forfeit, but the Communists missed it somehow.

Others died for their faith. In April 1971 one of the Christians received word that his wife's mother, father, two brothers and a five-year-old daughter had all been killed by Communists. The Khmer Rouge had captured 30 families living near Pailin and taken them deep into the forest, where the captives were held in a camouflaged stronghold, stocked with ammunition and rice. They were kept there for nearly three months; then one night the Khmer Rouge came and chopped Sou Pate to pieces with a machete.

Sou Pate was a well known Christian who had refused to take part in any of the local Buddhist ceremonies. His father, mother, five-year-old daughter and one son were shot dead, but the other son managed to escape, running for two days and nights in horror at what he had seen.

Alongside the atrocities of war God was at work. In April 1972 Stanley Mooneyham was allowed to conduct a three-day evangelistic crusade in Phnom Penh.

'When I saw half the people in the auditorium stand to accept Christ', he said, 'I almost sent them away. I couldn't believe they were sincere. Then I realised that they really wanted to know Jesus. I couldn't have stopped them if I had wanted to. I was astounded and shaken.'

Chau Uth marvelled: 'We feel that Phnom Penh has been shaken and turned upside down. Before, we were the hidden people, but now we are visible.'

On that first day of the crusade 6,000 people were

turned away because there was no room standing or sitting.
The crusade sparked off an explosion of evangelism as the
name of Jesus became known in the streets of the city. Dr
Mooneyham had also been allowed to make plans for the
opening of a Christian hospital, which would be a visible
mark of love and concern for the Cambodian people.

A singing group called the Danniebelles was allowed to
appear on Cambodian television, which until then had not
been used by Christians. The liberty Christians now had
stemmed partly from the enthusiasm and dedication of the
Cambodian Christians in caring for victims of war, but
most of all it showed how God was working. Many who
became Christians through the crusade were the means of
spreading the Gospel later.

One of these was a man named Sin Soum, who was born
in 1938 in a little village near Siem Reap. His father was a
peasant farmer with six children. The village was quiet and
peaceful, and each morning Sin Soum awoke to the sound
of the cock crowing. 'As a boy', he said, 'I wanted to help
people find a good way—a way of goodness.'

But suddenly Sin Soum's father and brother died, and
Sin Soum went off to study in a Buddhist monastery, where
he learnt much about the religion of his people. It failed to
convince him, and he was still unsatisfied when he became
a teacher. At the age of 22 he met and married Kao Long,
a young, attractive Cambodian girl, and moved later to
Battambang, where he was horrified by the poverty he saw
and began to study agriculture. After some time in
Battambang he took his wife and their six children south to
Kompong Speu, but increasing terrorism forced them to
become refugees. They moved to Phnom Penh to begin a
new life.

Life in the capital was depressing, but as Sin Soum sat
reading his newspaper one day he noticed a heading: 'Hear
the Good News for Cambodia told by Dr Stanley
Mooneyham.' He cheered up and went along to listen, but
was one of the 6,000 turned away. He returned early the
next day and made sure of a seat.

It was all new to him. He was deeply impressed by the words 'Jesus is alive, and wants to bring life and peace to every Cambodian' — and even more impressed when the speaker gave new meaning to an ancient Cambodian legend.

Sin Soum knew the legend well. It was that a great battle would take place where four rivers meet, and at that time a god will come with scars in his hands and feet and sides. He is called the Samartre, or a god of peace, and he will reign for a thousand years with equality and justice. Phnom Penh is a place where four rivers meet: the Tonle Sap and Bassac rivers join both arms of the river Mekong.

Sin Soum went home from that meeting a Christian, and because of the change in her husband's life, within a short time Kao Long became a Christian too. Sin Soum had embroidered on his shirt the emblem of a fish — the symbol of the early Christians.

The crusade was a revelation to many, and the Christians marvelled at the response. The Cambodian Evangelical Church was eager to follow up the people who professed faith in Christ, as over 600 had made decisions while a further 369 were listed as inquirers. Nobody had expected such interest. Young people had come to the crusade disillusioned and had returned home with new hope.

Minh Thien Voan was amazed. 'I tried to get in to see the meeting, and one young man wouldn't let go of me. I thought he wanted to see the programme; so I kept telling him there were no more seats. But he said he didn't want to go in; he just wanted to become a Christian. So I led him to Christ right there.'

Another man who had to go home early from one of the meetings came up to Voan and said: 'I want to accept Christ before I leave.' Voan knelt with the man on the balcony, and he accepted the Lord before the meeting had finished.

Merle Graven, the C&MA mission leader, said: 'This is the greatest thing to happen in all my years of service.' For half a century missionaries had been facing constant obstacles. The words of Stanley Mooneyham certainly seemed prophetic as he summed up the crusade: 'We are coming into harvest time. I have felt like a spectator, standing on the platform. It was the work of the Holy Spirit.'

The week before the second crusade, in November 1972, another singing group, the Palermos Brothers, visited 19 high schools and sang to more than 22,000 students. The crusade, entitled *Way of Peace*, opened with Son Sonne as interpreter and Lim Chheong as chairman of the planning committee. The crusade team was an international one, with Archbishop Marcus Loane of the Anglican Church in Sydney, Australia, and Dr Chandu Ray, an executive director of the co-ordinating office for Asian Evangelism from Singapore, taking part. 'We were amazed at the response we saw among the Cambodians', they said.

Chhirc's brother Huong had been offered scholarships in France and England, but in the end he went to the Philippines to train with Campus Crusade for Christ, who said he was their most gifted worker. Huong had dedicated his life to reaching others with the Gospel, and was involved in student and literature work at the *Way of Peace* crusade. Asked what he felt were the obstacles Cambodians faced in coming to Christ, he replied: 'The first is tradition, and the second disillusionment with the political system, leading to a feeling of general hopelessness.'

Those who were changed totally through *Way of Peace* found their disillusionment replaced by hope in Jesus Christ. To stop one young man, Chan Sokha, going to church, his mother hid his clothes. So Chan Sokha hid his clothes first, and because his mother couldn't find them, he got to church! His one desire had been to own a Bible, and so he began working for the Bible Society, selling Christian literature door to door. 'The first people I approached', he said, 'were soldiers, and I was very afraid, because I thought they were going to take their guns and kill me. Instead, to my great surprise, they accepted the Bibles gratefully.'

A wounded soldier who became a Christian at the crusade witnessed in the hospital where he was a patient, earning himself the nickname 'Jesus Man'. When he went home his sister was always locking him out of the house as a punishment for becoming a Christian. But in May 1973 he was baptised, and that month he led eight other soldiers to the Lord.

Over 10,000 people came to the second crusade, and by the end of the year there had been nearly 4,000 recorded decisions for Christ. Those missionaries who had been associated with Cambodia over the years felt like spectators. Before their eyes, the light of the Gospel they had nurtured was becoming a spreading flame.

6 The Spreading Flame

In Phnom Penh the main church, Bethlehem, was led by Kru Bun, who had as a young soldier dedicated his life to Christ during the Issarak rebellion. One Sunday morning at the end of 1970, Kru Bun preached with great fervour on the feeding of the five thousand. Vividly, he described Jesus lifting up the five loaves and two fishes, blessing them and then breaking them in pieces before handing them out to the multitude. He concluded: 'For the Church to grow it must be separated, and then God will multiply.'

Christians throughout the city were busy with a plan to put Christian literature in every home. Yos Oan, Son Sonne and Sonan had begun going through the boulevards of Phnom Penh, while Chhirc had instigated a plan to hold Bible studies in different homes to reach out to the officials of the city. 'If no-one comes I will go to them', he said — but people began to come. During two months nine people accepted Christ, and three of these were people Chhirc had contacted.

The deserted Vietnamese church became a meeting place for 200 children whom Yos Oan was keen to reach with the Gospel. A missionary remarked: 'Perhaps this is the beginning of a new church.' Within a few months it became Bethel church, and in the same month Bethany opened. At the first service in the three churches numbers had risen dramatically and this was just the beginning.

A handful of Cambodian students out of a group of 100 learning English became Christians. At lessons they often laughed and did not seem too interested in Jesus Christ, but one night the airport was bombed, and the sky reddened as all but two planes were destroyed. It was a steadily

50

worsening picture for the Lon Nol government, and the students who came for their lesson the next day were not laughing. Two tracts had led one young student to ask how he could become a Christian, and Kru Bun showed him the way of Peace. Everywhere people were asking: 'Where can peace and hope be found?' The C&MA missionaries felt that Jesus was with them and were unafraid, but it was a sombre thought that communication with the outside world was severed.

An officer issued this call to his men: 'I will not force you or coerce you, but I ask you to serve your country—to save your country from the enemy. I ask you to work giving no thought about hours, for the enemy has no hours. He is always at work.' They replied: 'We will serve with you and we will go with you—and if necessary we will die with you.'

Within Buddhist Cambodia, superstitions flourished. Priests sewed written prayers into their skins, and spirit mediums influenced many lives. But now, alongside all this, there was an obvious turning towards the Gospel of Christ, and the Holy Spirit was moving in a remarkable way among Cambodians. In Kampong Cham, people said: 'Jesus Christ must be very good, for he cares for his own and they are not afraid.' And a Buddhist priest lectured his students: 'Why aren't you like the Christians? They go out and evangelise, and everywhere there is interest.'

A Cambodian popular artist, Mr Hay, was converted along with his wife, who was very ill with a heart condition. Son Sonne paid a visit to their elaborate, ornate home one day and found that Mrs Hay was looking for the true Way. Both husband and wife responded to Son Sonne's light-hearted question: 'Why do you wait to become a Christian?'

After praying, the couple began to clear their home of lucky charms and idols. They even dug up a bush in the garden, because it had been planted there to guarantee their having many friends! Their shop, cleared of the paraphernalia of their former life, displayed alongside the magnificent pictures Christian tracts and leaflets—and their business prospered. Mr Hay bought a car, which he

gave to some of the Christian leaders to be used in
Christian work. He just had it on Sunday, so that he could
ferry people to church.

Mrs Hay was a radiant Christian, and in the short time
before she died she brought to church many women she
was friendly with. After her death Mr Hay continued to
work for Jesus, telling everyone about his faith, and one
night he had a particularly vivid dream. 'I saw Jesus on the
Cross, weeping for the world', he said. 'And as I watched I
found myself weeping too.'

The numbers enrolling at TaKhmau Bible school were
increasing, but it was still not easy to be a Christian. Some
families were very antagonistic to those who departed from
the Buddhist way. At a Bible study one troubled teenager
said: 'My father burnt my Bible after the last Bible study.
He does not want me to come any more, but I want to
come now that I am a Christian.'

Some, however, were admired because of their faith and
beliefs. When a general's wife was complaining about the
unfaithfulness of husbands, Chhirc replied: 'We Christians
are not like that. We enter into a contract for life, and we
trust each other and are faithful to each other.' The
general's wife was so impressed that when she met Bophana
she said to her: 'You are a very lucky woman, because your
husband loves and cares about you. When my children
grow up I want them to marry Christians, for then they will
have faithful husbands who will care about them.'

At the Russian-built hospital in Phnom Penh there lay
many victims of war. Chhirc, Bophana, Pastor Nou Thay
and another Christian decided to visit the wards, and the
scene that met their eyes was nothing short of chaotic.
They saw overcrowded, noisy wards and corridors, and sick
people jammed side by side, with their families surrounding
them. The misery was reflected in faces of complete despair
and agony. The Christians handed out tracts and cans of
milk, and during their first visit, one young soldier
accepted Christ as his Saviour.

Keam Ny, a young, vivacious girl, began visiting the

hospital, and she led a girl to Christ. As she was talking with her she noticed that three of the doctors were listening; so she invited them along to her church. They all promised to come.

When Keam Ny next visited the girl, she found that she had been telling others about Jesus. Several of the staff came to listen to Keam Ny talking, and one asked her: 'Why do you believe in Jesus?'

'How long have you got?' asked Keam Ny, laughing.

'We have about thirty minutes at lunchtime.'

'Well, I could talk about Jesus all of my life and still never finish', she said.

In that ward alone, four people asked to become Christians.

World Vision had plans to build a Christian hospital in Cambodia, and Chhirc and Minh Thien Voan helped them, although director Stanley Mooneyham had many critics.

'Why do you want to build in a place where buildings are continually being devastated by war?' they asked. He replied: 'A Christian can't wait until he is guaranteed safety and security before he reaches out the hand of love.'

On the day the contract for the hospital was signed a doctor accepted Christ, and everyone felt that this was God's confirmation that the hospital should be built as an expression of the love and compassion of Christ. It would be staffed by C&MA medical missionaries and Cambodians from the churches.

Son Sonne, who was director of the Cambodian Bible Society, was a dynamic evangelist. When nine people were baptised one day in April 1971, six were people he personally had led to the Lord. That same month a new church was commissioned at Ton Nop Tuck, and people began to worship there. A man called Ty Ruang, a member of that church, was unable to read; so he took out tracts on to the streets and asked people to read them to him. Several people became Christians by reading to him the tracts he obviously knew by heart!

One young girl who studied English came to the Halls one day and said: 'I want to die. I have just heard that 20 of my relatives have been killed in my village by rockets.' The war brought great misery to many, and there were many tragedies in and around the so-called heavenly city. Yet the Church was growing fast. Campus Crusade leaders who visited Phnom Penh for a training course said: 'This is the first time in our experience we have had more people going out on the streets to witness than have actually attended the course. It is remarkable.' In one day over 100 accepted Christ. Son Sonne's brother-in-law Seng led a taxi driver to the Lord while travelling in the vehicle with several other people.

Nou Thuoch, a brother of Nou Thay, was getting out of a cyclo* when the weatherbeaten old man pulling it asked him: 'Where are you going?'

Feeling a bit awkward, he replied: 'I am going to Bethel church.' Then he felt the conviction of the Holy Spirit, and he told the old man: 'Jesus Christ can bring you happiness and peace. Would you like to come with me?'

The cyclo driver did so, and at the end of the service he came to Thuoch and said: 'I want to become a Christian.' Thuoch told him to go home, read the tracts and pray, and to come back in a week's time if he was serious. A week later this wizened old man returned, and became a Christian.

Another missionary couple, Dean and Esther Kroh, came to Cambodia in August 1972. Dean was a trained doctor, and Esther had many years' experience in nursing. They had both been in Africa for 20 years, and had also just completed three years of medical work in the United States. When they arrived in Phnom Penh the new hospital had not yet been built; so they visited the refugee areas, where the noise of gunfire was constant and soldiers were everywhere. Barbed wire enclosed the camps, and many there showed the haunted faces of malnutrition. The Krohs

---

*A type of rickshaw pedalled by a man.

To learn more about the Cambodian people and find out how you can help, fill in this card and post it today.

I am concerned

about the Cambodian people and want to know more about them and how I can be involved.

Please send me your bi-monthly magazine.

Name: . . . .

Address: . . . .

. . . .

. . . .

HELP

is urgently needed .....

- — for refugees in Thailand.
- — for refugees in the West.
- — for those left in Cambodia.

HELP

is being provided .....

- — through relief supplies, medical aid, clothing, self-help projects.
- — through Christian literature, cassettes, visitation & evangelism.
- — through prayer and intercession.

HELP

SOUTHEAST ASIAN OUTREACH

help the Cambodians with your prayers and support.

Do not affix Postage Stamps if posted in Gt. Britain , Channel Islands or N. Ireland.

SOUTHEAST ASIA OUTREACH

FREEPOST

SWINDON

SN3 6BR

Wilts.

began working in a different camp each day, and their afternoons were spent, out of the sun, learning Cambodian with Keam Ny, who was now at TaKhmau Bible school.

While the Krohs were working in the camps among the pigs and other animals, in dirt and squalor, Keam Ny's father, Pastor Kong, came and took services there. Keam Ny spoke to the soldiers guarding the camps and brought other Bible students with her to talk to the refugees and give out literature. Hannah, Lim Chheong's beautiful wife, acted as interpreter for the Krohs—before rushing home to feed her baby.

Hannah had been adopted as a small child by a Christian woman. The woman's own children did not grow up to follow the Lord, and this was a source of great grief to her, but she rejoiced in Hannah, who always put Jesus first.

Lim Chheong, besides being director of the Bible school, was pastor of TaKhmau church. Refugees were flocking into the area, and Lim Chheong and Hannah had a special ministry to them.

One refugee, grief-stricken, told Lim Chheong: 'I am from Kratie, and I was really wealthy, with many rice fields. Now I have nothing. I am just poor and a refugee.' With pity Lim Chheong told him: 'You know life is like a flower that fades, but Jesus Christ will never fade or change, and He can bring eternal life.'

One of the most common questions was: 'Why do you care for us? You are not related to us.' The answer was: 'Because Jesus cares for you, we care for you.'

International help organisations were now coming to Cambodia, and they too were overwhelmed by the deluge of human suffering.

Many refugees were part of tribal groups. A Rhade tribesman who was also an Army officer and a Christian worked among them, spreading the good news of Jesus Christ. Ksor Koh, who spoke several languages, one day visited the Halls with a man who had as a boy been given a tract by Ed Thompson in Kratie province. Ksor Koh, whom they had never met before, told them of his escape with another Christian after they had been stranded in enemy territory.

'For 20 days we lived on leaves and fruit, until we reached a clearing and saw the Communists were a short distance away', he said. 'We crept into a village and found a Vietnamese family who welcomed us and made us a large meal of rice. In the evening they gave us a light and directed us to another house, where we were told we could sleep. But neither of us was happy there; so we decided to move out quietly and sleep instead in a derelict house on the edge of the village. The following morning we discovered to our horror that if we had slept where we were told we would certainly have been killed.

'Then we saw an Army lorry enter the village with some American soldiers on board, and in full view of the village we walked over to them and asked them to take us to the capital. In the daytime the Communists were disguised, and to the soldiers it looked like any other sleepy village, with children playing in the streets.'

Then he added: 'Did you know the refugees coming into the city at this moment are from Mondul Kiri province?' This was the very area that Ed Thompson had wanted to work in many years before, but had been refused permission. Now they were coming into the city, and there was plenty of opportunity to teach them the message of the Bible.

Ksor Koh brought 30 of these refugees to church the following Sunday, and soon there was a rapidly-expanding church among them. The missionaries often preached there.

Once Hannah was riding in a taxi which kept stopping to pick up more passengers. She was wearing a colourful sarong, and had on her lap a copy of *Four Spiritual Laws*, which attracted the attention of an Army lieutenant. 'May I have a look at that booklet?' he asked. She agreed, but when they reached the Bible school she asked for it back. 'I'm afraid I haven't another copy', she said. The lieutenant wanted to keep it; so Hannah persuaded him to go with her to TaKhmau Bible school, where 'there may be another copy.' Eagerly, the man went with her. At the Bible school Lim Chheong spoke to him, and by the end of the afternoon the lieutenant was a Christian.

Merle Graven wrote on December 12th, 1972: 'Our churches are all full. Our problem is to find ways and means of opening new centres. Buildings aren't always available; so anywhere, even the open air, has to become a meeting place to spread the Good News.'

Of 250 families living near the Bible school as refugees, 116 had become Christians.

After only six months as Christians Sin Soum and Kao Long, his wife, made a momentous decision. They went to live in a desolated area of the city which was soon to become known as the 'New Phnom Penh'—not at the call of a dead Buddha, but because of faith in a living Saviour. In that area the family of eight were isolated. They even had to erect their own palm tree hut as shelter from the sun and tropical storms, and each day Kao Long walked for 15 minutes to reach the nearest water supply. Danger was all around them: fleeing refugees often passed their hut. Kao Long called out to them: 'Come in here! Our God will protect you!' Some stopped, and soon there were other shelters being built close by.

One old lady grabbed hold of Sin Soum and said: 'Teacher, don't leave us tonight. We are afraid and want you to stay.' With his beautiful smile Sin Soum replied: 'Granny, don't worry. I have a friend who has lots of men, and He is going to place them on guard all around us.'

The old lady, with great surprise, looked round. 'I can't see anyone. Where are they?'

So Sin Soum told her about Psalm 91: 'For Jehovah is my refuge. I chose the God above all gods to shelter me. How then can evil overtake me or any plague come near? For he orders his angels to protect you wherever you go.'

They all slept well that night.

In their new home Sin Soum and Kao Long studied the

Bible with their neighbours. The Khmer Rouge were burning and pillaging villages on their relentless route towards the city, and many refugees began to settle in 'New Phnom Penh'. The Cambodian Evangelical Church and World Vision erected shelters for the newcomers. Soon there were 30 believers, and many more came to ask: 'What is this Christian Way?' Sin Soum became known not only for his beaming smile, but also for his contribution to the relief programme in the capital.

Within nine months Horeb church was built by Sin Soum, and people began to worship there, including a widow who lived next to the church. As a refugee she was terribly poor and, having no husband, she found it even harder to survive. Her main problem was getting water, and so she asked the Christians: 'Will you pray for me, that I can get water quickly?'

They all prayed about her water problem, and some began to dig a well for her. They had gone down just two metres when water gushed forth. Everyone was amazed, for normally at least ten metres would have been necessary. To that widow the water was a real gift from the Lord — so its first use, the following Sunday, was for a baptism service; 14 were baptised in the widow's well.

Meanwhile local rice was becoming unavailable, and rice was imported. Prices spiralled, and the poor were unable to buy on the black market. Thousands were trying to survive in the city. One agonised refugee told Sin Soum: 'We have been running for over three years, and people have taken us in, but this is the first time we have heard about Jesus, who has calmed our fears and brought peace to our hearts.'

A survey revealed that there were an amazing 17,000 orphans in Phnom Penh in October 1973. Minh Thien Voan and Stanley Mooneyham visited a group of 123 boys who were living together in a barbed wire enclosure. It was a barren place, and noisy with the sound of gunfire. Several boys were crouched around a cooking pot on an open fire. In the pot was a mixture of green beans and one little cut-up fish. The oldest boy was 14. Asked how he came to be there, one replied: 'My parents disappeared during a battle, and I became afraid and ran away to find my brothers and sisters among the refugees.' His story was repeated many times. It was a proud little boy who could 'use a gun and cook my own food.'

Soldiers, refugees, curfews and gunfire were just part of the fabric of life in Phnom Penh. The Cambodian nightmare was developing along lines that would have been unimaginable only three years before. One missionary commented: 'War is hell, but it often turns more people to God than peace.' That was never more true than in Cambodia.

7 Burning

A wrinkled Buddhist priest in a saffron robe sat talking to a
missionary, explaining how to become a Buddha. 'To
become a Buddha', he said, 'you must fulfil the perfection
of charity. This consists of giving your eyes more than the
stars and your blood more than the water in the ocean.
Buddha once sacrificed himself to a tiger in the jungle who
had no milk for her cubs, and was later reincarnated. You
must also give your body more than the surface of the
earth, give your heart, and your life.

'But the important thing is the fourfold truth of
Buddhism. That is that suffering is everywhere present,
and to cease from it is to extinguish desire, because it is
desire which is the cause of suffering. The middle way is
best, and that is to end suffering by avoiding extremes.
Where a Buddha has no desire for anything he becomes
meek, humble and lowly. Then he can be all-wise and
knowing, able to tell you even what you are thinking.'

The priest paused, and the missionary asked him: 'Have
you ever seen such a man?'

The priest replied: 'No, I have never seen such a man.'

A rumour had been circulating in the city that lightning
had struck the famous Phnom temple in early 1970, and
that this was an evil omen for Buddhism. Certainly, strange
things were happening. A Buddhist youth congress met in
1973 with the aim of combating 'outside atheists'. Over one
thousand young people attended, and at one session a
student asked: 'Why don't Buddhists tolerate other
religions?'

The speaker replied: 'We don't object to other faiths.' He
continued: 'Christianity is the only religion of any real
value. I have a Bible, and I have read it. You simply

cannot read what the Bible says and believe that Jesus
Christ was just an ordinary man.' Over half the audience
raised their hands when he asked how many there were
Christians.

A deeply distressed Army lieutenant met some young
Christians selling literature in the market one day, and
asked them: 'Have you got anyone older I can talk to?'
They took him back to Bethany church, where he told an
older man his story: 'Today I received news that my wife
was beheaded when Communists reached my village,
because I was a soldier.' The Christians wept with him as
he broke down and cried. They offered him the comfort of
Jesus, and he began coming to the church regularly.

One of the young teenagers who had gone out on to the
street to tell others about Jesus was taken to the police
station for questioning. 'Who told you and taught you
about this Way?' he was asked.

The boy replied: 'God taught me.'

'No, I mean who taught you?' repeated the policeman.

Again the boy replied: 'God taught me.'

'How much are you being paid?'

'Nothing. I am sharing this good news because I am a
Christian. That's what God has done for me.'

Of six churches that sprang up in Phnom Penh, five were
started by laymen in refugee areas. Their buildings were
sometimes made only of thatch, but congregations numbered about 300.

Dean and Esther Kroh had moved to a pleasant part of
the city called Tuol Kauk, about five miles from the centre.
But they soon found refugees moving in, and Son Sonne
was quick to pay them a visit. 'Could I hold a meeting in
your house?' he asked.

At the first meeting eight came — a young housegirl and
another missionary's housegirl, plus Son Sonne's family.
Esther was then evacuated to Thailand because the situation
in the capital had once more become critical. The
Americans were pulling out of the war. One frequent
visitor to Cambodia wrote: 'I saw refugees by the thousands

who had recently fled the terrifying scenes of battles. Bewilderment and confusion clouded their normally happy faces. I saw children by the hundreds who had been turned into homeless orphans overnight. As I beheld the sufferings of the gentle Khmer people I had a hard time believing that part of the world was saying, "Let's wait and see if this little country can survive."

'The news media showed pictures of grief-stricken remnants of a war which daily made people homeless. Cambodia didn't look as if it was going to survive. Boys of 12 to 14 were enlisted to fight, as men became difficult to count on. To escape enlistment some became Buddhist priests. Lorries stopped in the streets and men were picked up by soldiers in a war no one wanted. The army was ill-equipped, and despite the fact that 54,000 tons of bombs had been dropped on Cambodia, defeat was in sight.'

Five male C&MA missionaries remained — Merle Graven, Norman Ens, Gene Hall, Jean Jacques Piaget and Dean Kroh — along with the Wycliffe couple, Tim and Barbara Friberg. Constant bombing shook their houses and made sleeping difficult. They all met together to pray, and the Cambodians, undeterred, continued to proclaim the Good News. A group of Gideons from Bethany went out and visited the front line soldiers, and it was their boast that as the enemy ringed the capital with forces, they managed to ring the city with Scriptures. The soldiers, deserted by almost everyone, were eager for a message of hope.

Once more, miraculously, the enemy was driven back, and the Christians saw this as a respite given them by God, so that they could continue to preach the Good News. For politically the outlook was black. One young believer voiced the thoughts of many: 'I fully expect one day to be behind bars for my faith if the Communists come to power.'

From Bethany church another group of women visited the hospital, and a third group went out on to the streets to distribute literature. Although the sale of other literature was forbidden at this time, the Bible could still be sold. On one Sunday alone in the city churches 26 accepted Christ. Merle Graven was asked by students at the Buddhist University to speak about Jesus, and students and priests were given copies of the Scriptures.

Men Ny Borin, now Judge of the Supreme High Court, gave his testimony at Bethany church that month: 'My life is like the match and candle. The Bible is the match that finally came in contact with my life, which is the candle. Now I am burning for Christ and am a light in this world.'

Esther Kroh soon returned to Cambodia with the other women missionaries, to find that 'the church in my house had tripled, and people had overflowed on to my lawn'. Her housegirl, Kim Nyol, whose husband had gone off to Laos, leaving her with three small children, had made a firm commitment to Christ and had begun teaching Bible stories to the neighbourhood children. She held classes on the front lawn out in the hot sun while the church in the house spilt out into the back garden. Without any training Kim Nyol told stories with such an impact that the children listened eagerly and brought their friends along. Old Christmas cards were used as prizes, and on the lawn the children learnt to sing and pray.

One day a Cambodian mother brought her sick baby to the Krohs' house. Dean and Esther tried to save the baby's life, but it died on the patio. The heartbroken mother came to the church service, where Son Sonne's message was: 'We shall meet with joy our loved ones in heaven.' In tears, the woman came to Christ, but when she missed the next few meetings Esther became anxious and asked Kim Nyol what had happened to her.

Surprised, Kim Nyol told her: 'She lives a mile and a half from here, and has asked Son Sonne to take services in her own home. That is why she has not come.' So the living organism of the Church spread. From the meeting in the Krohs' house, four other fellowships sprang.

About half a mile from the Krohs' home was the very heavily-populated refugee area of North Dyke, where Son

Sonne had been asked to start a service. There were 18 at the first meeting, and the second time the number had doubled. Several weeks later 500 were meeting there, many of whom had never heard the name of Jesus before. Soon there were 700, and when some moved to another area, they took the Gospel with them. Four other groups sprang from this large meeting.

Near Pochentong airport was another overcrowded camp, and the Krohs had prayed that the Lord would provide an opportunity to speak about Him there. Many months passed, but one day Sin Soum came to see them with a man and his epileptic son. 'We gave the son medicine which controlled his epilepsy', said Dean. 'Then in gratitude he became a Christian.'

The man lived near the airport, and he too became concerned for the camp. One Sunday afternoon they held a meeting in the Catholic Relief Kitchen, and soon the place was filled with eager, noisy listeners. At one service 50 people were baptised. Then someone complained to the authorities about the noise. So the Christians began walking a mile and a half down the road to another place where they could worship.

In the September Todd and DeAnn Burke arrived in Phnom Penh, and later formed the Cambodian Charismatic Christian Mission. People poured in to listen as they held a crusade in the Palace of Sports arena, which they were allowed to use free of charge. An American group, the Luminaires, sang to those who came to hear about a God who could both save and heal. They also appeared on Cambodian television; many became Christians, and several received healing. One young man visited the Burkes and told them: 'My right eardrum was badly damaged through firing cannons, and I could not hear anything. During one of your meetings I touched my ear and raised my hand to God, and I could hear. Now I want to give my life to Jesus and study His word with you.'

The follow-up Bible studies were well attended, and 90 per cent of those who came became Christians. Soon a

Cambodia was a
staunchly Buddhist
country

Students at Takhmau Bible School

Fifty new Christians at the Open Air Baptism in January 1975
(Chhirc at bottom left)

service of baptism was held on the roof of the Burkes' house in a pool, and 42 men and women were baptised.

Helping the Burkes, besides Pastor Kong and Nou Thay, were young men like Sam Oeurn and Kong Saran. Sam Oeurn came to Todd one day and said: 'I have just been visiting a neighbour, and a girl there is in an awful state. She looks just like the cases of demon possession in the Bible.

'She was engaged to a man, but her father wanted her to marry someone else, whom she didn't like, and she refused. This man was so angry that he went to a Brahmin witchdoctor, who put a spell on her. From that very day she acted strangely, even trying to kill herself, having convulsions and screaming out, "Someone is beating me!"'

The family clearly needed help, and so Sam Oeurn and Kong Saran went back there. 'You must get rid of all your idols and incense', they said, and read to them from the New Testament. The mother wanted to become a Christian, but as she prayed the girl began to cry out: 'Leave us alone! Leave us alone!'

Sam Oeurn turned towards her and said: 'Leave her, in the name of Jesus Christ.' The girl quietened, and then asked for something to eat.

Those watching were amazed, and more asked to become Christians. But as soon as Sam Oeurn and Kong Saran prayed, she became restless again. In a trance-like state she spoke in English — a language she did not know: 'I respect Jesus Christ, but Sam Oeurn is not a true follower of him. I am the chief of the demons of Phnom Penh, and I wear the red scarf.'

Perplexed, Sam Oeurn left the house and went back to see Todd, who told him: 'This is one of the tricks of Satan. He lied to you. I'll go back with you.'

When they arrived, the girl became worse. Todd, in a commanding voice, said: 'We are the disciples of Jesus Christ, bought by the blood that defeated Satan, and through the power of the Holy Spirit we have been given authority over all the works of Satan and his demons. We therefore command you to leave in the mighty name of Jesus.'

The demon in the girl cried out: 'I'm leaving, just give me time! Bring back the witchcraft, and I'll leave.' With a loud cry it left her, and the girl sat up, saying: 'What happened to me?' Bible studies were held every day, and on the Sunday the girl, now completely whole, related a vision she had had: 'I tried to drown myself, but before I could I saw Jesus come, lift me out of the water and take me to a pleasant place where I had never been before.'

It was with great joy that she was baptised, along with 80 new believers. Soon a new Bible school was opened, and from there students went out into the city to witness.

At TaKhmau Bible school the students were now coming from a variety of backgrounds. Some were poor, and some had sacrificed careers to serve the Lord. One of the latter was Trieu Saree, married with four children. He had been comfortably settled in an insurance company when he became aware that God was leading him to go to Bible school. He had no money to live on if he went, but he knew that God would supply his needs.

As he sat at the table with his wife one day, there was nothing to eat but a bowl of rice, and he had one riel* in his pocket, yet he was sure the Lord would provide for his family. Suddenly the door was pushed open, and their two-year-old son came rushing in. 'Daddy, the dog has a riel in his mouth', he said. Behind him was their dog, and in its mouth not one riel—but a 100-riel note. God was honouring his servant's faith.

Many of the Bible students were also working and teaching in the many church groups, and the few pastors often worked in two or three churches. The Christians were coming from all strata of society. Once mainly rice farmers, they were now soldiers, teachers, businessmen, refugees and students. It was a church that had overcome all social barriers—where the rich mixed with the poor. Tradition and status meant nothing when Christians shared everything they had.

*Cambodian currency.

8 Death Trap

'My dear Tutor:

Please excuse me for I had not answered you immediately when I received your letters and the four preceding lessons. It's very difficult to explain to you. The high cost of living is growing from day to day, I can't live in this situation. I prefer to die but I think of my two children who are yet little, you know, my dear tutor, I earn only 1900 riels per month and I must pay more than 1000 for rice. I have nothing sufficiently to eat with the rice, because I must also pay every month more than 400 for the doctor. Now I never take breakfast . . . I start to think to philosophy, to Jesus to read the lessons you send me. I become such a fool if I always think of my luck. Please answer me as soon as you can, my dear tutor, or I will die.'

This desperate letter to England showed that the Cambodians were rapidly losing hope. But this man continued to correspond, and later he wrote: 'As bombs fell round about me I prayed to Jesus to protect us, and our house was safe.'

Living hope and confidence in Jesus could replace despair. Correspondence courses were in keen demand in Cambodia, and English lessons were increasingly popular. Many were influenced in favour of Christianity as they learnt English through reading the life story of Jesus. Others listened in to radio broadcasts from FEBC Manila, and like Yos Oan came to a point of faith in Christ.

A Buddhist school teacher marvelled as he listened: 'What a wonderful thing I used to listen to every evening over the air! Your talk, song, way of explaining God's word and about Jesus Christ, the unique Saviour of this changing world, are really the things I admire and I am in need of to live among people throughout the world. I should like to tell you I am very much excited when all my attentions concentrate on your broadcasting, and I would like your programme to last for ever so that I can know in detail God's words.'

This man had never seen a Bible. He had just listened to the radio, and was eager to know more. Students and young people walked around the streets of the big cities carrying small transistor radios which became more and more important to them as transport to and communication with other parts of Cambodia became difficult and dangerous.

Cambodia was making headlines. Perhaps not as big ones as Vietnam, whose war had dragged on for so many years, but the toll of human lives in Cambodia was attracting the attention of the world.

Pene Key was a determined, enthusiastic doctor whose powerful personality helped her to overcome obstacles that others would avoid. She was on holiday in Scotland, recuperating after ten years' intensive medical work, when she received an urgent telegram from World Vision. Would she head a team to Cambodia?

Her reply, unhesitatingly, was yes. She went to Cambodia, into a panorama of human misery, in October 1973. The World Vision team consisted of two nurses and two Cambodian trainee nurses, and they were visiting refugee camps like O Bekaam, with its 6,000 people. They set up a Red Cross dispensary there, and in other places nutritional day-care centres were started. One three-storey tenement building housed 900 women and children. Five families lived in one room, and for every 300 people there was one toilet. The team worked six days a week, and treated over 100 people a day. There was no let-up: the work went on growing until it reached alarming proportions.

The church relief committee, World Vision, the Catholic Relief Services and other relief organisations, such as the Red Cross, were all drastically overworked, but the people kept coming. Next door to the military prison there was a group of refugees in the half-completed Cambodiana hotel. Built originally for tourists, it had wide, spacious rooms, but there were no tourists now: it was no longer a very healthy or restful place.

City hospitals were jammed with the sick and maimed victims of war, and surgeons worked all night, wondering when the stream of casualties would ever stop. Pene Key visited a camp for discharged, handicapped soldiers and instituted a health programme. The Cambodiana clinic had an X-ray unit and a laboratory, and the worst cases were referred there. At Tuol Kauk nutrition centre pitiful scraps of children — suffering from protein and vitamin deficiency — appeared and were nursed back to health. In the midst of the tragedy the words of Dietrich Bonhoeffer had added relevance: 'To provide the hungry man with bread is to prepare the way for the coming of grace.'

After an unusually loud barrage of shells one missionary couple raced out on to the street — to face a horrifying sight. Two hundred bodies lay, ripped and torn by the mortars, scattered over an area of about a square mile. There was only one house left standing in that area, and it belonged to a Christian. Five babies were rescued — to be adopted eventually by American and British families. The heavenly city was turning into a death trap.

Norman and Marie Ens were well aware of the dangers. One day a rocket fell outside their house while Norman and his two sons were standing at the gate. Then a second rocket hit a passing car and shrapnel sailed over their heads, killing a woman who was standing in a high block of flats looking over the city.

The missionaries chose to live with danger, but they were rewarded by the growing response to their message. People were turning to Christ in ever-increasing numbers. And there was a peace in their hearts that was hard to explain in a city under attack.

The Holy Spirit was certainly at work. On the night before Chhirc Taing left Britain to return to his homeland he wrote a letter to a friend, urging people to pray that the Holy Spirit would 'do a mighty work out of the ruins of my country.' Back in Cambodia, he wrote: 'I thank the Lord for giving real opportunities to serve Him among our people at this time of harvest. Hungry souls have poured into our 15 churches in the capital each week, and there has been a shortage of Bibles for many months. We are running out of almost everything here, but not of the sweet love of Jesus, our dear Lord and Saviour who is manifesting himself mightily in our land.'

Chhirc had been busy not only with his Army responsibilities but also with his work for World Vision. He was on the executive council of the Khmer Evangelical Church, and involved with child care at Bethany.

Christmas Day 1973 brought a concentrated attack on the city. The missionaries there drowned the sound of guns by playing loud Christmas carols! Bethany Bookshop had put on a special display of Christian literature in several languages, and many people, including Buddhist priests, bought Scriptures: 75,000 pieces of literature were sold, exceeding everyone's expectations. The paradox of the Christmas message of peace in the turbulence and hatred of war-torn Cambodia was a striking one.

A woman from Sin Soum's church had a vision in which she saw a gold ladder with silver rungs. At the top of the ladder was Jesus, and Sin Soum was halfway up the silver rungs, calling and encouraging people to continue climbing. Sin Soum said: 'To me the ladder was my house.'

When the missionaries preached at Sin Soum's home they saw many turn to Christ. One week Jean Jacques preached and 15 were converted. Then Gene Hall went along and retold the story of the raising of the Widow of Nain's son. The floor was packed with adults in their brightly coloured sarongs, and children gathered at their feet. All were aware of the power of God pervading the atmosphere, and at the end 50 people came forward and accepted Christ. Two people cut off their devil strings, and five requested, and received, prayer for healing. 'Never before have I sensed such a response—it is certainly of God', marvelled Gene—one of the few missionaries who spoke fluent Cambodian.

Another Sunday, after he had preached at Horeb church and a further 20 accepted Christ, everyone went outside to watch the fighting, which was just two kilometres away. Smoke was billowing skyward as burning houses came under rocket attack.

In all sections of society there was a growing interest in the Gospel. The man who wrote the Cambodian National Anthem—Mau Vinna, a professor at the Buddhist University—became a Christian after studying one of the correspondence courses. He wrote: 'Before studying the course I was a simple believer in God. Frankly I was not sure that God could help me. Having finished Lesson 6 I now know many wonderful things about Jesus. Since I believe deeply in God I feel very strong in my heart, for I am sure that He loves and protects me in all circumstances. I don't even fear death any more. Daily I used to smoke two packets of cigarettes, but thank God now I have stopped. Day by day I find happiness and joy growing in my heart. Because of God I now have hope, help and a good life.'

Keam Ny married a Filipino Christian in 1974 and moved to Manila in the Philippines. There she began producing Cambodian language programmes. Later Lim Chheong and Hannah, with their family, went there too, and they began helping to produce good quality recordings. It was an answer to prayer, for the programmes used previously had been old, and repeated many times.

The Cambodian dry season, December to May, always saw an increase in fighting; when the rainy season arrived roads became impassable, and there was a lull in enemy activity. The early months of 1974 were therefore filled with violent clashes and resulting casualties. But the number of churches was still growing. The Chinese churches in Cambodia had begun a major outreach in 1972, which had brought many into the churches to attend English classes. There was also an International Church in the capital.

Pastor Kuch Kong invited one of the young TaKhmau Bible students (who were still working in the city and helping the churches) to the home of his relatives. It was March 1974, and he had been working with the Charismatic Mission. Sixteen people were waiting to hear what he had to say. He spoke for a while, but as they began to pray the owner of the house rushed upstairs and opened a door. 'I smell smoke!' he called to his startled guests. 'Look! My spirit house is on fire!' And he threw the box out of the window.

Kuch Kong interrupted the excited chatter. 'The Lord has done this to show you that you are not even to have them in your home, as they are the instruments of Satan', he said. 'All you need is Jesus.'

The fear of the Lord made many get rid of their idols that day.

An identical thing happened when a young Christian began witnessing one day to a soldier outside his tent. The soldier prayed, accepting Christ into his life, and suddenly the spirit box inside his tent burst into flames. The power of the Lord was everywhere evident.

9 Circle of Crisis

The Chinese character signifying 'crisis' is made up of the two parts 'opportunity' and 'danger'. The Cambodian crisis contained both elements. The Khmer Rouge, in their efforts to 'liberate' the people in the dry season offensive, were continuing to press forward as government forces retreated. Occasionally there were government victories, and when that happened the victorious general would go riding proudly into a city—perhaps only on a motor bike! The death and injury rate seemed unbelievably high, but the Army had little to fight with.

For those living in the cities there was little work, and one of the worst enemies was time. Boredom and rumours flourished, destroying morale, and to escape the tedium many young people began learning English. English Bible classes were packed with people who came simply out of curiosity, but with the passing of time their curiosity became genuine interest, as they discovered how much Jesus cared about them. Interest and belief began to coincide, and more and more turned to the Christian Way.

An Indian preacher, Subodh Sahu, spoke at the annual conference of the Cambodian Evangelical Church, emphasising the need for Christians to come to God in prayer, and to walk each day with the Lord. Over the next few months the same message came from many sources. Over 100 were baptised, and the growth of the Church had some striking parallels to that recorded in Acts. In May 1974 three new groups formed, one of which began as a Sunday school class and later had a congregation of 100.

Son Sonne was preaching in an area of the city known as North Dyke, and by the end of the year there were 1,000

Christians there. These people formed four groups, and Son Sonne arranged for a lay person to lead them in their services. He was also holding a Bible study group and wanted to have services with them. In Phnom Penh he had to get permission, and so after prayer he visited the local district commissioner, who said: 'Of course you can have permission. I became a Christian myself about three months ago. If you want to, you can also build another church there.'

'The harvest is so ripe that no longer is there the need for plucking', wrote one missionary. 'We gather the fruit that has fallen of its own accord.'

Kuch Kong and his wife moved to the prosperous town of Pailin, near the border with Thailand, in March 1974, and although there were only a few Christians there, they soon realised that the Lord was moving among them. The Church began to grow as new believers were added to it.

The youth centre which opened in Phnom Penh became a popular place for young teenagers. Many missionaries helped there, taking Bible classes. Trieu Saree, the deputy director, lived there with his wife, family and chickens. In the garden the teenagers planted vegetables. One of the Bible students who spent his holidays at the centre said: 'At the centre we worked, lived and ate together with joy. From my sharing and teaching others, I also learned myself.'

The missionaries who taught in the centre saw many come to the classes — some through eagerness to learn English. Rose Ellen Chancey, a young, vivacious, dark-haired missionary with OMF, taught the Genesis story of creation, and 60 people came to hear it. Ruth Patterson, of the C&MA, a Canadian woman who had spent 19 years in Zaire, began a class especially for Buddhist monks, where she taught the life story of Jesus Christ.

Later the centre became a church.

Ravi Zacherias, an evangelist who had trained at Ontario Bible College, came to conduct a crusade at Battambang that year; he also took some meetings in the capital.

Battambang was the place where the first Christian Evangelical Church was established. Over 1,000 turned out to hear him speak, although five out of the seven meetings were conducted in pouring rain. During the crusade a teacher who had been in a Buddhist monastery for 18 years was converted, and many joined the Church. Samuel Mok, pastor of the Chinese Church in the town, had held a 5.30 a.m. prayer meeting before the crusade, and afterwards the churches in Battambang flourished.

A school teacher working with the Charismatic Christian Mission went to live in a small village called Andek Hep, near Battambang. He began witnessing to those around him, and he soon had some angry Buddhist neighbours. They wanted to get rid of him, and made his life very difficult. But one day a man came to see the teacher and said: 'Will you pray for my wife? She has been paralysed for two years.'

The teacher went immediately and found a large crowd outside the hut. They stood watching as he said: 'Jesus, heal her and confirm your word.' At once she was healed, got up and walked, and the crowd fell back in amazement. Eager voices began to ask: 'How can we become Christians?'

Every evening the teacher held Bible studies, and a small church was formed. When Todd Burke arrived with Bibles he found that many had begun a new life in Christ.

At Kampong Speu some Bible school students were giving out tracts and preaching when a blind woman pushed her way forward through the crowd and stumbled up to the speaker. 'Can Jesus help me to see?' she asked. The student stopped speaking and said: 'Yes, he can. Lord, please help this lady to see.' Immediately she began shouting: 'I can see! I can see!' Again, as a result many became Christians.

Reach Yea, the pastor of Ton Nop Tuck church and president of the Cambodian Evangelical Church, took Norman Ens to visit people who had been contacted through Christian radio broadcasts. At Siem Reap seven people had become Christians, but there was no church.

They visited 30 people taking correspondence courses, and 15 became Christians. Soon a house meeting was begun.

At Pursat four people began an English reading course, advertised through a local newspaper, which gave lessons based on the Gospels. But again there was no place of worship. Then a teenager, Phoutar Hau, who had committed himself to Christ at the youth centre in Phnom Penh, became concerned for his parents, who lived at Pursat. He had studied the Bible, and he said: 'I found it new, good and interesting for my life; so I received it gladly. The Bible became my one and only favourite thing. Before, I could not stop doing bad things. With God I live in warm peace but without Him I am like a sheep without a shepherd, wandering alone in a desert. I have already decided to follow God and do His will. I can sleep soundly every night. Many temptations trying to poison me have been beaten, and their attraction is nonsense for me because of God's power.'

Phoutar Hau began helping translate the TEE* course *The Shepherd and His Work,* but he wanted to share the Good News and so decided to return to Pursat. Carrying as much literature as he could manage, he set off for his home. Nothing was ever heard of him again. Two weeks later the city of Pursat fell to Communist forces.

One of the girl students at TaKhmau Bible school returned home to Kampong Chhang and led her mother to the Lord. A team distributed Christian literature there, and the students also went into dangerous areas in the provinces. At Kampot, near the South Vietnam border, they met in a badly-damaged church, repaired it and began to worship there. The previous pastor, an ex-Buddhist, was now a missionary in South Vietnam; so the students took the services. There were about 100 believers there in 1974, and numbers seemed to grow as the war worsened.

Theological Education by Extension began in December 1974, with 30 students.

The last crisis was fast approaching, and the capital was full of fear and rumours. At Christmas the Cambodian Evangelical Church held a pageant in the Olympic stadium. Chhirc had got permission to put on a magnificent display, with stalls created by the Phnom Penh churches showing scenes from the Old and New Testament — from Creation to the Second Coming of Christ. Thousands came, and Christmas Eve and Christmas Day saw many added to the Christian churches.

The Angel Christian Orphanage run by Jimmy Rim was expanding all the time. Each child had a tee-shirt with *Jesus loves you* printed on it, and Jimmy used to say confidently: 'The Lord won't call me home until my children have been cared for.' At the orphanage the children occasionally held all-night prayer meetings, when there was only one rule: 'All children under five must go to bed.'

One sad day Jimmy rescued a little girl called Sarey in a crossfire between Communists and government forces. He ran to her through the bullets and brought her back to safety, blood pouring from her wounds. The little girl was in a state of shock — not only from her wounds, but also because she had just seen her parents, brothers and sisters killed. Jimmy took her to the hospital, where her leg was amputated, and she later joined the other children at the Angel Christian Orphanage.

By now the Mekong river was blockaded in at least three places, and the stranglehold on the capital was making flying in to Phnom Penh extremely hazardous. Among the Christians there were few who had not lost at least some of their family through the war, and many viewed all suggested solutions to it with mistrust and fear. Incidents like the firing of a resettlement village built by World Vision, where many refugees had tried to rebuild their lives, did nothing to allay fears for the future.

Many Christians from that village moved into the city and began living in tents. The spirit of sharing was something that Cambodians were learning all the time, and it made them a richer community spiritually. Working and worshipping with the Cambodian Christians brought a blessing to those who were privileged to know them.

Leaving them was a hard decision to take, but time was running out.

10   Hunger for Life

A boat in an open field symbolised the moving of the Holy
Spirit in Phnom Penh. A young believer from Bethlehem
church offered the boat for use as a church building, and
soon it held a congregation of nearly 100.

Noah's Ark was a big old wooden craft standing dry-
docked in the middle of a field. Inside, on the bottom
floor, eight orphans lived among the chaos, while upstairs
children and adults crowded in to listen to the message of
Jesus Christ, and to sing and worship the Lord. The
Christians were keen to meet wherever they could, and
nobody was waiting for a building to go up before starting
a church.

A brother and sister were converted and began telling
the rest of their family about Jesus. One of the other
brothers, Keat, was a sailor—an officer on a ship at
Kompong Som, Cambodia's major seaport. First, Keat got
a visit from his brother. 'You must believe in Jesus', he was
told.

Keat was angry. 'I am not interested in this Jesus. He is
not true. All I want to do is make money.'

Then his sister, who was very beautiful and kind, and for
whom Keat had a great admiration, came from Phnom
Penh to see him. 'Brother', she said, 'you must believe in
Jesus, for your money will not last, and when you die you
cannot take it with you.' She pleaded with him, but Keat
would not listen.

'This Jesus cannot be real', he told her sharply. 'How can
you believe in the Bible? I want to have a good life now and
make lots of money and see the world.'

Sadly, his sister replied: 'No, brother, that is wrong, for

one day you will have to answer for your sins. Please read the Bible, and then pray and ask God if He is real to show you Himself. But if you leave it too long, it will be too late, and your chance to repent and have a new life in Jesus will have gone.'

Keat took the Bible and went to sea. Weeks passed, and then one day the ship began to roll badly as a storm blew up and a heavy fog engulfed it. The ship was on the edge of a fierce tempest. Up ahead they heard the distress call of another ship caught in the storm. The crew were afraid, and Keat, remembering his sister's words, went to his cabin to read the Bible. The storm got worse, waves covered the deck and the ship seemed close to sinking. In desperation, Keat prayed: 'Oh God of my brother and sister, please save me as you saved them. Deliver me from this storm, and I will follow you.'

That evening the wind dropped; by the following morning the sky was clear, and Keat knew he must follow Jesus.

*   *   *

Phnom Penh was surrounded, but as there had been many false alarms and predictions of disaster, nobody was ready to call it a day. Instead there was uncertainty, and dread of the unknown. At the Tuol Kauk nutrition centre 75 children were being cared for, and many tiny children were unable to enter simply because there was no room. Pitiful little children, wasted remnants of a cruel war, lay in the heat, some with parents too poor to look after them, and others with no one even to think of them. Nurses were filled with compassion and distress at their condition.

The new World Vision hospital was nearly complete, the wards painted pink and blue, and linen and surgical instruments in place. The C&MA medical team—Mary Lou Rorabough, Lynn Walsh and Barbara Neath—along with the Krohs, were looking forward to the opening, but in the meantime they were training young Christian

Christian leaders and
missionaries.
Left to right:
Eugene Hall, Chhirc Taing,
Minh Tin Voan, at the back
Dr Cena Kroh, in the front
John Kwong, Son Sonne,
Andrew Bishop (holding
suitcase)

Jimmy Rim with
Cambodian children

Newly baptised Christians
at Aranyaprathet Refugee Camp,
Easter 1978
Insert — Pol Chhorn.

Cambodian Church in Paris

Cambodians as nurses. Twenty-four took the course, and during their training several were also baptised as a demonstration of their living faith in Christ.

The impact of the war was so horrifying that it was hard for people listening to the radio and watching television to believe that God could do anything in Cambodia. It was only a little country, with everything against it. Many were fleeing for their lives, but little was said about those who stayed to the end. For most Christians the refugee camps were just places where masses of unloved and uncared-for people slept; few knew that in those very lives, in people whose earthly possessions had all been wiped out, God was working.

Two young Cambodians, Keth and Thol, were visiting the overcrowded hospitals. They went through the wards and the corridors, talking to any who would listen, and then returned to the youth centre, where they talked and prayed for the crippled soldiers they had met. Keth rented an old truck and took some of the new believers from hospital to visit Sin Soum's church, Horeb. Many were carried out in the arms of the missionaries and Cambodians to the waiting truck.

Sin Soum received them in his overcrowded church with love and compassion. OMF missionary Don Cormack said: 'It was a memorable service, packed out as usual. Afterwards the Christians gathered round outside to talk to the men. One soldier was even reunited with his long-lost family, who were Christians at that church.'

The crippled soldiers soon had their own church—the *Amputees' Church*—in the house of a C&MA missionary couple, Andy and Beverley Bishop. Men who had felt defeated by the war found new hope in Christ, and shared it with others who joined them. Soon there were 100 meeting, and one of the most remarkable sights in Phnom Penh was that of the men who went out in wheelchairs and on crutches to tell others: 'Jesus is alive and can bring you hope.' They borrowed crutches to get to church on Sundays; one man even borrowed an artificial leg! Impressed, the hospital governor told Don Cormack: 'I don't know much about Christianity, but if it can transform my men like this, I want to know more about it.'

Jean and Roselyne Clavaud had been working among the refugees in an area known as Boeung Trabek. After his imprisonment by the Khmer Rouge, Jean had returned to the capital with a renewed ardour, helping with translation and working in areas with no pastor. He wrote: 'It is now more important than ever that Phnom Penh attends to the message of peace and the love of Jesus Christ. Everywhere there is great suffering.'

The New Year began with a 'magnificent fanfare' as the city rocked to the sound of explosives. At six o'clock on the first day of the year rockets began to land near the Clavauds' house. 'The fifth rocket was for us', said Jean, 'but it was diverted by the branches . . . . and also by an invisible hand.' In February 1975 the Clavauds left Phnom Penh with real regret; Cambodia had been their life for so long.

The following Sunday afternoon, a telegram arrived for the C&MA missionaries. It was from their head office—a directive that all 14 adults and four children should leave at once. All agreed, but with heavy hearts, for although they were aware of the advances of the enemy, they were also aware of what one missionary described as 'the precious moving of God, great spiritual advances and a new hospital all ready to be opened. We said goodbye to Cambodian Christians determined to live for God.'

The OMF missionaries were also advised to leave. The Cambodian Christians would be endangered if the missionaries remained, and even veterans like the Ens and Halls knew they had to go. Some who had not been in Cambodia very long also felt great distress at leaving. Those who had been there longest had known years of work without many coming to Christ, but they were now in the middle of a great explosion of faith, and there was agony in leaving so many behind.

When he left, Don Cormack wrote: 'Dear brothers, I

look forward to that day when there will be no longer wars, hunger, pain or separation. Separation—the word leapt from the page of this hurriedly written letter . . .

'He was leafing aimlessly through a very old copy of *Time* when I first felt compelled to go and talk with him, a timid young stranger sitting alone in the deserted classroom. I saw within his dark, sensitive eyes a depth of anguish which reached far back beyond that "happy day" when an unknown old man handed him a tract as he wandered late one evening along the bank of the Mekong, drowning in incredible problems of despair and loneliness.

'His village had been gutted, his family life torn apart and destroyed when "They" ruthlessly swept westward that dry season. Then came months of harsh indoctrination and an escape which led only to further daily struggle to stay alive and out of the way, alone in a besieged city overcrowded and disease-ridden, where two million others likewise struggled.

' "I loved Jesus immediately. I think it was His great compassion that touched me, and of course He knew all about it, and me too," he said.

'As the hot season began, and battle sounds from the shrinking city defence perimeter grew louder, Little Brother became increasingly preoccupied with the future.

' "What will we Christians do when the Khmer Rouge come?" The question pierced me like a sharp knife, as he raised his head. I recall mumbling simply: "God is faithful. He will take care of His own." And I thought as I touched his hand and his eyes slowly returned to the page, "Oh God, you must."

'With the prevailing intense spiritual hunger there were rich days of distributing tracts, witnessing on the streets and selling literature. One day in early January the team was moving among a great crowd gathered along the waterfront near the beautiful palace, watching bombs rain down on Khmer Rouge positions on the opposite bank. People were weeping, some having fled only the night before as villages were overrun and burned, relatives killed or carried off. For them there was no place to go that night, and some demanded: "Why doesn't your God do something about that over there, then?"

'Little Brother returned to our rendezvous shaken by the passionate outbursts which had rebuffed his shy advances. The little group prayed and encouraged each other then, separating again into twos, they went off the more eager to proclaim: "Listen, God has done something about that over there."

'By this time Little Brother, along with several others, ran a regular house meeting and found plenty of eager participants. There were still bundles of literature all over my room when, with one other close brother, we spent the last precious night together. We sat around the dim wavering yellow light of a candle and talked till sleep overtook us. He had also recorded the rest of my language book, "so that when you come back you will be able to speak our language", he said. As I recall, they were bright and happy, concerned yet noticeably possessed by a great peace.

'It was just as well that we had said it all the night before, because as the final day in Phnom Penh broke, sunny and hot as ever, words failed us. One by one those whom I had come to love deeply, had taught, worked and lived with, came into that little room for the last time. Unsuccessfully we each struggled to express our hearts.

'Finally Little Brother stood in the doorway, his head down. He was holding the potted plant that we had nurtured along from a little cutting. It was all he had asked for. "You won't forget us, will you?" he said quietly— lingered momentarily, then quickly turning, picked up a suitcase and led the way down to a waiting cyclo.

'I wept unashamedly because separation from these brethren at such a time was painful beyond words, and I was having great difficulty reconciling myself to the fact that I couldn't stay to suffer with them. It seemed to betray my whole love for them and purpose in going there.'

*   *   *

It was February 27th, 1975. The new hospital committee had met only once, with Son Sonne, Chhirc Taing and Minh Thien Voan taking part in the discussion of plans for the future. Now the future seemed bleak as the missionaries were evacuated, but they continued to pray for God's guidance. Chhirc sent a letter to his praying friends:

' "Where is the Lord God of Elijah?"

'This is also the cry of the young Khmer Church leaders at the moment. Elijah had been sent by God to the Israeli nation during the dark reign of its evil King Ahab. Despite the mighty miracles Elijah had performed, the people had not changed their hearts from sin. Then the time came for Elijah to be taken to heaven, and the young Elisha had to carry on the mission during those dark days in Israel. But Elisha's special request of God's power was granted. "The spirit of Elijah rests upon Elisha."

'Dear friends, do remember us in your prayers as we Khmer Christians are left behind to continue the task in the difficult days ahead. We do need God's greater power and wisdom, as Elisha did. Please pray for us and ask God to give us the right words as we boldly tell our agonising people about our Lord, and as we explain to them that His salvation is for them now. May God add many more souls to His young Church in the Khmer Republic, and let it grow stronger until the day of His return.'

Another Cambodian Christian wrote to Bangkok:

'No one can help our country only God. Please ask the brethren to pray for Cambodia and me in proclaiming in this situation. I believe this time is very different from any other time, so that we can bring the challenge of Christ to the people.'

The Christians became even more keen to reach out during those last weeks of freedom in 1975. Churches continued to expand as people saw the believers' faces radiating hope and confidence.

Trieu Saree wrote to Andrew Way in Bangkok:

'We are looking for you to come back and see how the Lord works in Phnom Penh. I received some money for

Bibles and will give them to refugees who are so poor in a new church in a small house which now is full up. We hear bad news about Cambodia every day becoming worse and worse with every hour. But the Lord says, "Peace be with you." '

There had not been many missionaries in Cambodia, but those who came were from many different countries and from different missions — British, American, French, Chinese, Indian short-term workers, a Korean, an Indonesian, a girl from New Zealand and some from Australia.

By February 1975 the Summer Institute of Linguistics team had expanded, and the Fribergs had been worshipping in the Cambodian churches as well as working with the Cham people. They had faced one problem after another. Whereas others had seen Cambodians eager to accept Christ, they had found the Cham people hard and unresponsive. Yet among the younger Chams there were many who were disillusioned with the hypocrisy of their Muslim leaders.

The Fribergs' language helpers, Haw and Dam, were — outwardly at least — practising Muslims. Haw was a generous, warm-hearted man married to a Cambodian girl. He worked most of the time as a school teacher, and gave away much of his wages to help refugees. Once as he was helping to translate the Gospel of Mark into Cham, he said to Tim and Barbara: 'Though I believe Christianity with my head I cannot become a Christian, because I am a Muslim.'

His words were prompted by the fear of persecution by the Cham leaders. He tried to follow the principles of Christ in his own life, but he remained blind to his own spiritual needs.

Dam was his cousin, quick-tempered and impetuous, but enthusiastic to help translate the Bible. One day, while he was working on the sixth chapter of the Gospel of Mark, he said suddenly: 'I am just like Herod. I really like to listen to you, to what the Bible says, but when I go home I am very perplexed.' Neither of the men would commit themselves to

Christ, though they listened and talked, as did many others among the Cham people. It seemed a barren field.

In the February the smouldering hostility of the Cham leaders erupted against the Fribergs. A group of the elders were having a discussion in public when Barbara and Tim arrived. One fierce leader glared at them and blurted out: 'If you do not stop translating the Bible, we will kill you or force you to leave.'

Everybody stopped and looked at them. In the crowd there seemed to be no friends. They had little choice but to return home, filled with dismay. Perhaps their work in the besieged capital was over. Bombs rained down everywhere, and no one knew where they would fall next.

They prayed, believing God would answer, and next day there was a timid knock on their door. On the step stood two of the Cham leaders. They said: 'We want you to continue to translate the Bible for us. Yes, we are Muslims, but if we are only Muslims because our fathers were, what kind of religion is that? We want to know the truth, and if you translate the Bible we can read it, and we can see if that is the truth.'

The Fribergs were filled with joy at this answer to their prayer, and knew that God wanted them to carry on, after most of the missionaries had left.

Barbara had produced a couple of Old Testament stories. One was the story of how the baby Moses was rescued from Pharaoh's soldiers, and the other was the life story of David. Tim had translated the story of Joseph. Together they did the account of the birth of Jesus, based on the Gospels of Matthew and Luke.

The Government had never allowed them to publish their primers, but they had printed 200 copies of the Christmas story and given 100 of these to Haw and Dam to distribute, as they knew they would have to leave by March. They never knew what happened, or even if Haw and Dam themselves made a commitment to Christ, but they prayed that God would use each copy of His word to show people the truth of Christ.

Poverty and hunger became widespread both in the provinces and in the capital as the Khmer Rouge tightened their grip on the cities, and planes carrying supplies became more spasmodic. But alongside all this, hunger for the Word of God was on the increase too.

11 Going Out

Phnom Penh was a dying city—suffocating slowly under Khmer Rouge pressure. The grim statistics of carnage reflected, through the headlines of the world Press, the agony and helplessness of a defeated people. The death throes of the city were watched on television, often dispassionately by people who could not believe it was real. It was such a 'horrifying trail of tears' from Cambodia to Vietnam.

In this mire of human misery Pene Key and the medical teams kept working. She wrote: 'I waved goodbye to a little Cambodian girl leaving her native country for her new home and family in America. Beside me my Cambodian doctor colleague said, "She is a lucky, lucky little girl. Why did she get chosen?"

'Today in my clinic at the Cambodiana refugee centre there were more than 500 mothers with their sick children waiting for their turn. Some will come again tomorrow and some the next day. I chose 200 to 300 children from among them. The rest are the unchosen. There is agony for me in this choosing. When I call to my doctors and nurses and clerks, "That child is the last one for this morning", what am I doing or saying to the child after that last one? The anguish of the mother whose child is refused haunts me and my staff. Her face stays with us as we eat our lunch, knowing that she is waiting and watching her child.

'Sometimes a waiting child dies while I am away resting. How then can I rest or eat or sleep? How can I not choose to see that child? Why did I choose to stop at the child before that one? If I had chosen to see one more child, that child might be alive today.

'This morning there were 34 children needing admission to the hospital. There were only seven empty cots. I had to choose. 27 critically ill children went back home in the arms of their despairing mothers . . . How do I choose which one? All these children are God's little ones. He loves and cares about every one of them. I believe He wants every one of them to be cared for. He does not want me to choose one from another. He loves them all.

'I have a prayer I use. Lord, don't let me have to go on choosing which child.'

*   *   *

Jimmy Rim had to visit his mother in Korea, because she was seriously ill. When he tried to return to Phnom Penh he found he could not get a flight. He never saw his orphan children again. The World Vision team made trips to the orphanage, and the Cambodian Christian staff looked after them as well as they could, but time was running out, and the future did not bear thinking about.

Stanley Mooneyham was questioned about the new hospital, which was just about finished. He was asked: 'It looks as if it will never be opened. What have you to say to that?'

He replied bravely: 'All I know for sure is that I believe God. I'm just not convinced that God is through with Cambodia. Our investments are not guaranteed, but we were never told to be sure our investments were safe before we got involved. We are told to do one thing, and one thing alone — trust.

'I would say this. With 26 newly-founded churches in Phnom Penh alone, and a group of believers that numbers around 10,000, I would say that we have already received our dividend. If we had to leave Cambodia tomorrow, and even if we never occupied the hospital, it would still be all gain.'

Pene Key lived in an area of the city known as Rocket Alley, near Army headquarters and therefore a prime

target. She worked unceasingly and earned herself the title
of Good Doctor. On March 12th she flew out of Phnom
Penh to get further supplies, and to rest after days without
sleep. Nobody thought she would go back into that hotbed
of human disaster, but she told one reporter: 'I have to go
back. My job is not finished yet.'

When she did, she was greeted by long queues of
desperate people. Her Cambodian team now had 150
workers, and she was impressed by their dedication and
loyalty. One of her helpers, who became her friend, was
Minh Thien Voan. Working unceasingly to help relieve the
suffering of others, he refused to leave Cambodia and its
problems — as did other Cambodian Church leaders.

On the same day that Pene Key flew out of Phnom Penh,
Chhirc sent a letter. 'The Church here is very active, giving
God's message through the official radio stations and
asking people to fast and pray. The response has been
good', he wrote.

Stanley Mooneyham had, on March 2nd, paid his last
visit to Cambodia. 'I could come and go', he said. 'I had a
passport to get out. But for these Cambodians there was no
escape hatch. If the government fell, they would remain
under a new regime. When the rice was gone they would go
hungry. If their homes were attacked they would bury their
dead.'

Bewilderment, fear and hopelessness were stamped on
many faces during those last few weeks. Chhirc expressed
the suffering of Cambodia in his own words in a further
letter:

'Our land has become a desolate wasteland. Our streets
and our homes lie in silent darkness each night from 7 p.m.
At daytime there is fear of danger. Rockets fall right in the
city centre, killing people and destroying shops and houses
almost every day. Many people have deserted us.

'This is the situation of Phnom Penh in March 1975. It
reminds me of Jeremiah 9.12: 'Oh that my eyes were a
fountain of tears. I would weep for ever. I would sob day
and night for the slain of my people. Oh that I could go

away and forget them and live in some wayside shack in the desert, for they are all adulterous, treacherous men."

'However, there is the only hope for our future, in Jeremiah 31.3-5: "For long ago the Lord has said to Israel, I have loved you O my people with an everlasting love; with loving kindness I have drawn you to me. I will rebuild your nation. You will again be happy and dance merrily with the timbrels. Again you will plant your vineyards upon the mountains of Samaria and eat from your own gardens there".'

*   *   *

A small boy was brought to the nutrition centre by his mother, who started working there in gratitude for the way the nurses cared for her sick child. The father had been killed in a rocket attack, and two weeks later tragedy struck again. The mother, too, was killed by an enemy rocket.

The nurses were heartbroken. One of them, Sandra Menz, decided: 'The little boy is an orphan. I cared for him when he was sick, and fell in love with him. There is no way I am going to leave without him.' In the chaos of those last weeks she filed for, and was given, adoption papers, and the little boy became Simon Michael Menz at the age of ten months. They left Cambodia to start a new life.

Intense fear gripped many as tragedies multiplied. The World Vision nurses were also aware of the all-pervading panic, and one wrote: 'Nothing so disturbs our rest and takes away our peace of mind as physical and spiritual fear. If there was nothing to fear, half the unhappiness would be taken out of our lives. Our Lord, who wished the best for us, that we might be full of joy and peace, would have us altogether free from fear. Not only have we this loving command, "Fear not", but we are graciously given a threefold reason for obeying this Divine injunction: "I have redeemed thee, I have called thee by My name, thou art mine." We are His, the One who died for us. With His

wonderful words ringing in our ears we can fearlessly face
the unseen future, knowing that it is in His hands.'

*   *   *

Chuck and Sally Kellar had come to Cambodia in November
1973, and after a year of Cambodian language study they
went to live, with their two small children—John, 3, and
Jodie, their adopted Vietnamese child, in the Pailin area.
They made contact with the Brao tribal group, and despite
the danger they felt a great urgency to preach the Gospel.
They also began helping with the people's medical needs,
although they had no medical training.

There was no shortage of opportunities for talking to the
local people, who were anxious to know why the family had
come to their dangerous village, and the weeks passed in
telling others the Good News. There was tension as they
gathered to pray. Food and communication lines were
being cut, and the eventual decision to leave, when there
was so much to do, was a painful one. But the Khmer
Rouge were closing all exits.

Chuck wrote: 'I think you ought to know, dear brothers,
about the hard time we went through in Asia. We were
really crushed and overwhelmed, and feared we would
never live through it. We felt we were doomed to die, and
saw how powerless we were to help ourselves—but that was
good, for then we put everything into the hands of God,
who alone could save us, for He can even raise the dead.
And He did help us, and saved us from a terrible death.
Yes, and we expect Him to do it again and again.'

Forced to leave Pailin, they said: 'It made us think how
many Bible characters were forced to move out.' On March
14th they headed for the safety of Thailand, with heavy
hearts and a deep burden to pray for those they had left
behind.

*   *   *

The deterioration of Phnom Penh was shattering. Some of

the male C&MA workers were able to get back into
Cambodia for a short visit, and they were deeply shocked
by what they saw. Homes and offices lay blackened and
devastated, and misery was everywhere. In that decaying
city of violence, smouldering rubble littered the streets, and
the teeming crowds were restless. People wanted to get out,
but there was no way. The Mekong was blockaded, roads
were cut, and the airport was under constant fire. So Gene
Hall was amazed when he visited the Christians.

'In contrast to the bleak military and political situation,
there was an entirely different mood in the Church. All the
churches in Phnom Penh were filled and overflowing. The
Sunday of March 30th there were 185 persons who turned
to Christ in the city churches. That same week saw 135
persons follow the Lord in baptism. Inquirers were coming
to the churches and homes of Christians daily, asking about
Christ. Also another new church was started in a home,
making about 29 church groups in Phnom Penh*. The zeal
for evangelism was only intensified during the month of
March.'

In the city young people had been visiting homes, and
rallies were held at which many came to Christ. The
departure of the missionaries was a clear indication that
the end was near, and on Good Friday the Cambodian
Evangelical Church leaders met together at Chhirc's home
in the city. Together they took communion, and afterwards
Chhirc, who had once been so proud, took a basin and
washed all the others' feet — the first time that any
Cambodian Christian had performed such an act. They
read from John 13, and spoke quietly about the future.
One said: 'I believe that for some of us there will be death.'
Others agreed, and together they prayed and prepared
themselves for the days ahead.

Sin Soum and others received threatening letters from
the Communists, but they continued with their work
undeterred. When some were asked to leave because they

*Not including Charismatic groups.

stood in danger of elimination, one replied: 'We cannot desert our people. If we leave, who will take care of them? They will be like sheep without a shepherd.' The Church chose Son Sonne and his family to leave and help reach out to Cambodian refugees in other countries, but in the end he was unable to get a flight, and so remained behind.

The Charismatic Christian Mission had also seen growth in its churches. Maranatha, where Pastor Nou Thay worked and preached, had a congregation of about 300; it was a thriving fellowship where God had revealed His presence.

Todd and DeAnn Burke had to leave Cambodia at the end of March, taking with them five children for adoption abroad. They fully expected to return but, like others, they could not get back into Phnom Penh. 'We felt just like refugees. We had nothing to show that we had even been to Cambodia.'

Nou Thay cabled them, 'The Church is well and prospering,' and DeAnn said: 'It seemed then that once more the words of Hudson Taylor were relevant, for the scaffolding had been taken away and the rising building was clearly seen!' Their Bible school was full of young people training to tell the message of Jesus, and they knew that God was with them there in Cambodia.

In Pailin, just eleven days before the fall of Phnom Penh, God's presence was made very clear. The 13-year-old son of Ton Kham, a faithful elder of the church, died after a week-long fever. The parents took his body, 'cold and stiff', to the church for the funeral service, to be conducted by Kuch Kong. But before the service began, the congregation prayed.

The service was about to start when San Kong's wife let out a high-pitched scream: 'I saw the boy's fingers move!' She pulled off the covers and put her hand on his chest. 'I felt his heart beat and the body grow warmer', she said. Minutes later the boy stood up, and the church held a praise service instead of a funeral.

To the believers there it was a tremendous demonstration

of the reality of God's presence, and many committed themselves in a deeper way to the Lord.

Two days later Kuch Kong got on his motor cycle and went to visit Sam Oeurn, who was working with his wife Youvanette in Battambang. Sam Oeurn told him: 'Last night I dreamt a terrifying dream. I woke up, and then later slept and had the same dream. In the same night I had the same dream three times.'

'What was your dream?' asked Kuch Kong.

'I dreamt that I was lifted up over the city of Battambang and was looking down on it,' he said. 'The enemy began to advance, moving into the city, driving people out into the countryside. Then the city had nobody in it. Everybody had to go—the old and the young.'

Sam Oeurn was deeply troubled by the dream, and asked the Lord: 'What does it mean? Is it going to happen soon? Is it really going to happen that way?' And as he prayed the Lord told him: 'Yes, this will happen soon, and you must prepare the Church.'

So Sam Oeurn gathered everybody together on the day that Kuch Kong came riding over to see him. Kuch Kong was impressed—it was not the first time that Sam Oeurn had foretold future events—and he returned home and told his own congregation of the vision.

Within ten days the city of Battambang was overrun, and everyone was driven from the city like cattle—just as the dream had foretold.

On April 7th Chhirc sent a letter from Phnom Penh: 'Jesus is alive, isn't He? And so are we over here in Phnom Penh, amid rockets and electricity and food shortages . . . Today we failed to have our hospital dedication service. The Lord willing, the work there will be carried on. Please continue to ask God to bless us and His work among the Khmer people as a whole. Much work, as you know, has to be done. The Lord is with us, isn't He? And we praise Him because we are not on the losing side.

'Many souls are hungry for God's word. Please pray for us as we keep on serving Him in Cambodia in all circumstances. May many hundreds of thousands of souls be saved by the grace of our Lord Jesus Christ.'

Ksor Koh had been sent on a course to America, leaving his wife and family behind. Seeing the desperate situation in Cambodia, he asked American Christians to pray that she would be able to get out, as he could not get back in. He was desperate, and it looked impossible.

On one of the last flights out on Tuesday April 8th, the plane began to develop engine trouble as it was preparing to take off — a not-too-pleasant experience with rockets landing close by and the noise of gunfire and explosions ringing in the passengers' ears. Stanley Mooneyham was on the plane, and so were Minh Thien Voan's wife and family, en route to Bangkok.

The tension grew. Then, running across the runway, came Ksor Koh's wife and three children. Her papers had just been cleared, and she was rushed out to the stranded plane and bundled aboard with her children. Immediately the engine trouble vanished, and the plane took off.

Pene Key flew out of Phnom Penh for the last time on the same plane, taking with her 23 very sick children for adoption abroad. Her team of Cambodian doctors and nurses stayed behind, but a peaceful settlement to the war was no longer a possibility. Newspaper reporters also stayed a little longer. One was a Christian called David Aikman, who worshipped at Maranatha church, where Nou Thay told him: 'My aim is to serve the Lord or die.'

The Lord was moving in a miraculous way through the churches of Phnom Penh. Everywhere numbers coming to the services increased. Nou Thay preached one Sunday shortly before Phnom Penh fell:

'In the first century Christians were persecuted, burnt, beheaded and thrown to the lions — but they did not stop believing. If 100 die, then 1,000 will be raised up — nothing can stop their faith, because they have strong hope that Jesus Christ is coming back, by the promise we have in Acts 1.10,11. When they die they will rise up when Christ returns. If they are alive when He returns they will go with Him.

'Not only in the first century were Christians persecuted, but all Christians everywhere, any time, any century. There are always those who persecute them. But where there is trouble and persecution there is always growth.'

In those last few days Minh Thien Voan saw his family come to Christ; his parents and sister accepted the Lord. To his young wife, Theri, he wrote: 'I might have to die in Cambodia, but it is worth dying when my parents and sisters have turned to Christ. The next time we meet may be in heaven.'

Alice Compain, an OMF missionary, received a letter from her language teacher in Phnom Penh. Nyop was a 15-year-old girl who was led to accept Christ after an attack of typhoid which nearly killed her. She was now a confident, radiant believer, writing of hope and trust amid the wreckage of war: 'I am giving thanks to God at this time, when I read many verses in the Bible, and He always blesses and gives me great comfort. I am sure that the Lord is thinking about us right now, and He will never forsake us. I trust Him wholly for everything. All my hopes are in Him.'

Nyop's letter, and the letters of others, showed the faith, love and hope that was present in the debris of war. They stood as a monument to the great work God had done in Cambodia.

Phnom Penh fell to the Communists on April 17th, 1975, and all communication with Cambodia ceased. Sadness overwhelmed those who loved and prayed for its people. The future seemed grim for those who had remained behind. There had been growth and expansion, but what now? Was it to be death for the Church of Cambodia?

12 Border Road

'Leave Pailin at once and go to Thailand', said the Lord as Kuch Kong prayed in the early morning of April 17th.

Kuch Kong woke his wife and gathered the church together to share the message the Lord had revealed. Hurriedly, 25 believers packed as many belongings as they could carry and headed for the Thai border, a few miles away. They arrived in Thailand at the same time as the victorious Khmer Rouge were entering Pailin. Within hours the Communists had driven the people out into the countryside to forage for their own food, and to survive as best they could.

Just two days before Kong left Pailin his eldest son had arrived from another town, and he made the journey to Thailand with his father. The family was together, and safe. Keam Ny, their daughter, was also safe, helping with Cambodian language programmes in the Philippines.

It was a time of new beginnings. Prince Sihanouk in Peking was overjoyed and triumphant: 'Joy and happiness are so deep one cannot say anything. My passion is Cambodia. The glorious way it has emerged is my finest reward. My fate for tomorrow no longer interests me. What kept my flame burning is this goal which I have had for my country, which has now surpassed my hopes; because I have indisputably defeated the Americans.'

Relief was the emotion of others. The war had been savagely fought and won, and now, it was hoped, Cambodian would live at peace with Cambodian. Helicopters arrived in Thailand carrying high-ranking officials of the Lon Nol Army to safety. Some fled in cars and lorries, but most were content to remain and try to adapt to the change of government. But inside Cambodia there was silence and mystery, as communication with the outside world was shunned and offers of aid were rejected. The new Communist government wanted to do things its own way.

Fear was in the eyes of new arrivals at the refugee camps. Jimmy Rim paced to and fro along the border with Cambodia, grief-stricken, thinking of the fate of his orphanage children. His usually smiling face was clouded. Prayer was not an optional extra here, it was the place where he and many others sought — and found — answers.

As Job questioned God and discovered more about His splendour, majesty and greatness, so many had a revelation of Him at this time. For a week Jimmy sought the Lord in his deep distress, and then the Lord spoke to him, and he was changed immediately. He recounted a vision: 'I saw many adults being killed, but the children remained. I knew that in ten to fifteen years' time my children would still be telling others about Jesus.' With a new peace, Jimmy began to look again for unwanted children.

On the bridge into Cambodia, the black-shirted guards of the Khmer Rouge could be seen on patrol. Most were youngsters, brandishing their guns arrogantly. Missionaries tried to talk to them — sometimes successfully — over the barbed wire. One young soldier spoke of his family and village and accepted a Gospel of Mark.

Crowds were still crossing into Thailand, but soon the small border town of Poipet was left deserted as the professional Khmer Rouge forces moved in and its people, excited and worried, were moved into the interior. Soon Poipet was a ghost town; not even the sound of dogs barking could be heard in its streets. Only the Khmer Rouge soldiers remained.

Refugees brought stories of turmoil and chaos as hundreds of thousands of people, whether healthy or sick, were pushed out into the countryside. Rattling over the road to the frontier in June came the last of the foreigners, carried in trucks and dumped at the border. They confirmed that the forbidden land was the scene of a violent upheaval.

There had been a mass exodus of frightened and bewildered people, forced into the countryside from the capital.

'In Phnom Penh two million people suddenly moved out of the city en masse in stunned silence; walking, cycling, pushing cars that had run out of petrol, covering the roads like a human carpet, bent under sacks of belongings hastily thrown together when the heavily-armed soldiers came and told them to leave immediately.

'Everyone was dispirited and frightened by the unknown that awaited them, and many were plainly terrified because they were soft city people and were sure the trip would kill them. Hospitals jammed with wounded were emptied, right down to the last patient. They went out limping, crawling, on crutches, carried on relatives' backs, or wheeled on their hospital beds.'*

People went out not knowing when they would return. The city was emptied of all but those who were sheltered in the French embassy. Children were carried on the backs of their parents, or put in a type of hammock that others struggled to carry.

It was a horrifying sight. Men were taken away and shot as families were forced to keep on marching from the city. Rotting corpses were left on the sides of the roads, or in a corner of a field. No one dared ask why they had been killed. All the time the soldiers hurried them on impatiently, and to emphasise their point fired shots into the air.

Terrified and disorientated, the people moved forward, trying to head for places they knew. As they travelled on they began to abandon possessions which became too heavy to carry. Old people lay where they fell at the side of the road, and their weeping families moved on at the insistence of the soldiers. There was no help for the sick.

One refugee, Pam Moeurn, told his own story:

'On April 18th my wife, three children and I regretfully left our home and took the road going south. So many

---

*1975 by the New York Times Company. Reprinted by permission of the New York Times.

people jammed the highway that we crept along at less than half a mile an hour. We made barely three miles the first day. At different checkpoints along the way all the men identified as soldiers were taken prisoner. Their families were told to keep walking. When they questioned me I said I was a medic. They asked: "What kind of medic? Army?" I replied: "A Soviet friendship medic." Fortunately they did not question me further, and we went on to my wife's village. Along the way we saw many corpses of soldiers who had been shot; we did not dare stop and sleep.

'Finally on April 22nd we limped wearily into my mother-in-law's home at Takeo. When she saw me she burst into tears. "Son, you've escaped death only to face it again here", she said. Against all my protests the village head registered me as a military instructor and sent my name up to his superiors.

'A short time later my family and I were invited to a merit festival, but it turned out to be a political indoctrination session. Loudspeakers blared out Communist slogans. For three days we were forced to listen to the indoctrination programmes. Then 2,000 of us "liberated" soldiers were pressed into labour gangs to build a dam. The daily work schedule was from dawn to midnight, with short pauses to eat. No-one dared stop work, lest he be killed.

'On May 3rd another big freedom celebration was announced, for all the "newly liberated" who had arrived from Phnom Penh. Buses took us to a large Buddhist temple on the mountain. We were told to take our belongings and dress in our best clothes for the joyous occasion. For two days busloads of people arrived at the temple — brigadier generals, colonels, teachers, doctors, midwives, until there were 200 people.

'Not until we were locked in the temple and a guard was set did we realise the treacherous trick played on us. When we asked the guards what it was all about their only answer was, "You'll know tonight at the meeting." At six o'clock in the evening they began calling out a family at a time. No one inside the temple knew what was going on outside, but we were very apprehensive by this time.

'Two hours later they called my name. We roused our sleeping children and went outside. It was raining dismally. My wife went ahead, carrying our two-year-old son, and I followed with our two older boys, aged four and twelve. Suddenly a group of men armed with guns, bayonets and knives and carrying ropes charged out of the woods and surrounded us. As they tied our arms and blindfolded us I protested: "Why all this just for a meeting?" They retorted: "You're a soldier, and not to be trusted."

'When they tied my arms I braced them so that the rope would appear taut. Later I was able to untie the knot with one hand. Twenty yards further on we were stopped and questioned again: "What was your work?" I replied truthfully that I had driven military vehicles. When they questioned my wife about my work, she replied hysterically that I was a taxi driver.

'By this time we both knew we were facing death. The soldiers snatched the infant from my wife's arms, and she cried out in alarm: "No, let us die together." But they did not even grant this simple request. After bayoneting the child they stripped and gagged my wife before killing her. They then yanked my two older sons away and killed them in like manner.

'With my free hand I was able to lift a corner of the blindfold. Seeing the terrible carnage taking place, I made a mad dash for the woods. They shot 30 to 40 rounds after me, but by that time I was more fearful of their bayonets and knives than of their guns. I fell headlong into a dry stream bed, which hid me effectively from their searching flashlight beams. A hand grenade hit so near that dirt landed on my head. After walking right past my hiding place, they finally gave up the search.

'By midnight they had finished killing all their victims. As far as I know I was the only one of those 200 people to escape that night. By then the rain had stopped and the stars were shining. I crept northward, and by dawn reached the railway. My only clothing was a pair of black shorts, and I had no food. After several nights of walking and days of lying flat in the woods, I came to the home of an uncle. He advised me to try and make my way to Thailand if I wanted to survive.

'On June 6th I started my trek to Thailand. An Army colonel travelled with me, and we reached Siem Reap in two days. Red guards were patrolling the city; so we circled round Angkor Wat, the ruins sacred to every Cambodian. This was my first glimpse of these temples, and I wept when I saw the Red Flag waving over them. After several more narrow escapes and periods of forced labour we finally reached the mountains bordering Thailand—a welcome sight indeed! On July 19th, 77 days after my family was massacred, we reached Thailand and freedom.

'During the days that followed, memories of the terrible fate of my beloved family so overwhelmed me that I thought I would go insane. Then it was that I met the Lord Jesus at the missionary's home in Surin, Thailand. Wonderful peace and joy flooded my soul. Now when the thoughts of loved ones haunt me in the night I just pray to Jesus and He brings calmness.'

John Ellison—the son of David Ellison, one of the first missionaries to Cambodia—and his wife Jean had been working with the C&MA among Cambodian-speaking people in Thailand for 26 years. They were living at Surin, and it was in their home that Pam Moeurn dedicated his life to the Lord. Jean said: 'We had long wanted to work in Cambodia, but God had kept us in Thailand. Now God has brought Cambodia to us.' They began their ministry as the first helicopters landed, bringing out the Cambodian officers, and they knew that as fluent Cambodian-speaking missionaries God had given them the challenging task of telling the destitute refugees of the love of God for them.

At the beginning of the exodus the Thai government was not prepared for the flood of humanity that poured out of Cambodia, and it was a cause of great alarm when crowds of refugees began to cross the border. The Thais wanted, if possible, to trade with the new government, and they were afraid that letting refugees settle would hinder their chances of establishing links with the Cambodian regime. They solved the problem by restricting the newcomers to camps near the borders, and there, in primitive conditions, men, woman and children waited. It was the action of the C&MA, YMCA, Southern Baptists and other Christian groups that, in the words of the International Red Cross, 'averted a disaster'. They began to distribute food and clothing to the refugees.

In August 1975 a meeting was held at the C&MA guest house in Bangkok. Present were Thai officials, and representatives of the United Nations, the International Red Cross, missions and relief agencies. The first and every subsequent meeting opened and closed with prayer. Andrew Bishop, a fair-haired C&MA American missionary who had spent a short time in Cambodia, was elected chairman for the first year. The Ministry of the Interior gave permission for Christians to work freely in the camps, and the spread of the Gospel was once more evident as many refugees found new life and faith in the dismal, sometimes prison-like surroundings there.

At Klong Yai (Big Canal) camp Jimmy Rim had rented a house, where he lived with several children. He also taught about 300 children in the surrounding area, and went and told any of the adults who wanted to listen the message of Jesus Christ. The Gospel was proclaimed in the camp in five languages — Cambodian, Vietnamese, French, English and Chinese. During one visit by Andrew Way 133 Vietnamese and 180 Cambodians asked if they too could become Christians. News spread fast of the love of the Christians towards the refugees.

Jimmy's new family had also seen much suffering. One day, while Jimmy was visiting Klong Yai camp, two boys aged nine and eleven pushed their way through the crowd around him. They were accompanied by an old Vietnamese man who had been searching for Jimmy. 'These boys have no home, and their parents are in Cambodia', he said.

'They have been ill-treated by a fisherwoman and have run away from her. Can you take care of them?' Jimmy agreed, and the children came eagerly to the house, where they told their story.

'We were on a small island when the Communists took over. Our parents had sent us ahead of them, and they were going to follow with the younger children, but while they were on the wrong side of the river the Red Flag went up. We were separated and did not know what to do, as there was no way back. That night a boat came from the other side carrying Khmer Rouge soldiers, who shouted: 'Tomorrow we are coming to get you!' Many were very frightened, and we were too. So those of us on the island decided to flee in the boats.

'We waited until the dead of night and crept into the boats, careful not to make any noise. We set sail, and though many small boats did not make it to the shores of Thailand, our boat did — although we too faced death. We drifted by night until we reached the coast. Instead of freedom when we arrived we were enslaved by an old woman who kept us half starved and beat us. Now we have escaped and have come to live with you.'

These two found that Jesus was their friend, and took Him with them when they went to England, to begin a new life in a strange land — far from the tragedies they had witnessed.

A little boy explained what Jesus meant to him as he lived in the camp: 'I used to steal cakes, take revenge, get angry often and kill little birds. I didn't believe in Jesus because I heard that Catholics killed animals and people, and that Protestants were no different from Catholics. But then one of my relatives believed in Jesus. I asked him for a book about Jesus, and so I came to believe. I took my book to school, and six or seven of my friends understand about God now too. I know Christ has carried my sins in His body to the Cross. I don't get angry, kill, take revenge or steal cakes. I love Jesus and have a new heart.'

Young and old were seeking a new way of life in the

camps—tense, unhappy, overcrowded places where people sought frantically for news of lost relatives. Wives searched for husbands, husbands searched for wives, children looked for parents, and everywhere there were the signs of anguish and despair.

Inside Cambodia the believers, like everyone else, were being scattered, and it was impossible to know where most of them were, or even whether they were still alive. The fact that some were prepared to die for their faith was little comfort.

Cambodian Radio broadcasts boasted that theirs was the true Communist revolution—purer than that of China and Russia. Reports of killings and reprisals continued as refugees escaped. Atrocities were commonplace in that largely-forgotten area of God's creation.

One missionary wrote: 'As I think of those we knew and loved in Phnom Penh who were forcibly evicted from their homes and businesses into the countryside, I wonder: do they have mosquito nets to sleep under at night, medicines to soothe their sicknesses, pots to cook with, food to dispel their hunger, water free from infection, salt to make up what is lost in sweat in the tropical heat? Are the Christians experiencing God's miracles—comfort, peace, an open door to heaven, Christ's presence and power, and His angels' protection? How many more have been added to the Kingdom?'

13 No Way Back

'Do you know why I believe in Jesus?' another refugee
began his story. 'When I was a student in Battambang
province I saw a Christian going everywhere and telling
everyone who was living in the town about the New God.
Afterwards my friend and I wanted to protest to the
Christian who was telling the true story about God and
Jesus. We started to look for his mistakes, but we could not
find any, because he was a real Christian. He had a quiet
character and respected all the messages of God.

'On April 17th I was forced by the Khmer Rouge to work
very hard in the fields from morning to night. Immediately
I began to pray to God: please help me and take me away
from my miseries. I didn't know where God lived or what
He was like. I was confused by the Buddhist God—a
dummy made by man.

'One day I escaped from Cambodia to Thailand. When I
was in Kabinburi prison I met a man who had the book of
Genesis. I borrowed it from him and read it, but I didn't
understand, and I didn't believe. I didn't believe because
the book said that everything on the earth was made by the
Lord. . . . I thought that the human being was made from
a human being, the bird was made from the bird, the tree
was planted from the tree and that no one could make
them or create them.

'After I left prison I met Sister Rosa Brand (OMF) in the
old camp, and she gave me some books about Jesus. After a
few days I saw Soup Pho teaching the children, but I
thought he was mad. Afterwards I saw Christians having a
meeting and singing songs. I was very surprised. What did
they want to do? I had never seen anything like it before.

Also I had seen three English girls giving some milk to the children. They gave clothes and gifts to the new refugees coming from Kabinburi prison. Why did they do this? I wondered again. Was this the way of the Christian religion?

'One day when I had some free time I picked up my book that Sister Rosa had given me. I began to read it, but I didn't understand. In the evening I decided to go to a Christian meeting. By the end of the meeting I didn't want to joke any more. I felt happy, and little by little I began to know God and believe in Him. One day I remember going to the meeting when Andrew Way was teaching. He explained to us about the life of a Christian and the life of a person who didn't believe . . . I saw the light.'

*　　　*　　　*

Many now thought of the Church of Cambodia as dead and buried. A Swedish news reporter contacted Todd Burke while he was on a visit to Sweden and said: 'Well, all your work was a waste, wasn't it?' Todd replied: 'Come to the meeting this evening, and I will give you an answer.'

Todd wondered what the answer was for the Christians of Cambodia. He knew God had not deserted the Church, but how should he reply to the reporter's question? As he prayed before the meeting, the picture of Mary Magdalene pouring ointment over the feet of Jesus came into his mind. He read the story, and the words of Judas. Others had thought her offering an extravagant waste!

That evening he delivered (with the reporter listening) a sermon ringing with hope and confidence. 'The Church of Cambodia was anointed for burial, but not for death', he said. 'In the eyes of the world it was a waste, but in the eyes of God it is a fragrant offering to the Lord.' Whether it convinced the reporter Todd never knew, but it was certainly an answer to despair and hopelessness. Jesus was still with the silent, isolated Church, and their friends were safe in His care.

*　　　*　　　*

A Church was being formed in the refugee camps as small groups met and sang, prayed and shared what they had learned from the Bible. For several months literature was scarce, and the few available tracts were reprinted, and the copies distributed. Later a cargo of Cambodian Bibles arrived, hot off the Hong Kong presses, and soon funds for literature were flowing in from all over the world as the refugees responded more and more. There was no money to pay for Bibles, and so refugee believers committed to memory 30 verses to earn one. One young man received his Bible the day before he boarded a plane for France, having hurriedly memorised his texts.

Kuch Kong, the Cambodian pastor, baptised 71 new believers in July, and a further large group the following month. He was living with his family for several months in a camp at Chantaburi which was expanding rapidly. Tin shelters were knocked together to hold whole families, and these shacks provided protection from the hot sun and the sweeping monsoon rains. Heavy flooding made life even harder in some camps. Southern Baptist workers distributed dried fish and rice at Chantaburi and had an effective ministry in the area. All missionaries were amazed at the warmth of response from these people who had lost all they valued in life.

The camps were all guarded, and the people were trapped inside, waiting for a flight to freedom. But Kuch Kong continued to preach enthusiastically about the Way of Hope.

After the initial flood of refugees, small groups and individuals began escaping across the border to tell of the terror of their lives in the new Cambodia. They were just people of the land, disillusioned and bitter, seeking another piece of land where they could settle and raise a few chickens and pigs—but when they arrived in Thailand they found it was not so easy. Nobody wanted them. The Thai government would not let them settle, and other countries did not want people with little or no education; so they remained locked in a camp, unable to farm the land.

Despair and hopelessness were on many faces. Thailand had seemed a haven, but now, apparently, it was just a cruel illusion. They were totally homeless.

It was clear they could not go back. The Thai government, in a bid to discourage new refugees, had sent back a group of 26, including a boy of 11; all were summarily executed by the Khmer Rouge, and their corpses left in the open sun. No more were sent back.

But fear of being ordered back into Cambodia spurred many refugees to obtain papers that would give them entry to another country, and missionaries tried to liaise with the various embassies on their behalf. The United Nations provided money for air transport in many cases, but most had to stay and wait . . . and wait. Time dragged in the camps, and boredom became a disease. In their enforced idleness the refugees were unable to shake off their tragic memories, and they dwelt on the horrors they had witnessed.

Those who went to the USA soon after the fall of Cambodia and Vietnam found that people wanted no reminder of a war that had gone wrong. After all, it was a bad chapter in America's history. But the C&MA began a project to help refugees in the various American camps, and Rose Ellen Chancey, who had worked with OMF in Cambodia, was asked to go into Camp Pendleton and help.

'I look out into a sea of hurt, dead, hopeless faces, with the saddest eyes', she wrote. 'As they listen to the Good News, to the message of hope, I see heads begin to nod—and when they knock on my door to—as they say it—"enter into church" or "offer myself for Christ", beautiful smiles and beaming eyes break forth after they pray. Often I can hardly keep back the tears as I listen to their prayers, promising to trust, obey and follow Christ, and thanking Him for bringing them here and giving them peace.'

Rose Ellen found that in the three months the camp was used to house the Asian immigrants she was able to see the Holy Spirit at work again, as she had in Cambodia. Small miracles were taking place. Despair changed into hope.

Before going to the camp Rose Ellen had been on a short

visit home. Her family had told her that Cambodian soldiers were living nearby, and she prayed that she would meet them. Soon she did meet one—a young man called Bun Roeung. 'I had a dream', he told her with a smile. 'I dreamt that I would receive news from God. This message would tell me about how I could become a Christian.'

Rose Ellen was delighted. She told him: 'Only Jesus Christ can help you. You must believe in Him, for He died on the Cross and rose from the dead. He is the Son of God.'

Bun Roeung accepted Christ; soon two of his soldier friends came along to the church that Rose Ellen attended, and they too believed. The soldiers had no news of their families in Cambodia, but they knew they could not return, for return meant instant death. Their families had been driven from their homes, and they would not be able to find them anyway. They were lonely and sad, but the Christians made them welcome, and for one man there was a bonus. When Rose Ellen arrived at Camp Pendleton she met his wife and mother, who had managed to reach America, and the family was reunited.

On her first day in the beautiful camp at Pendleton, Rose Ellen met a couple who had become Christians through the ministry of Norman and Marie Ens. They introduced her to another Cambodian couple, who asked: 'Can we become Christians?' Two more Christians she met were a Bible colporteur's son and his wife from Phnom Penh. She was also introduced to an ex-film star who told her: 'While escaping from Cambodia I prayed, "Please help me, any god who hears!"'

Rose Ellen wrote enthusiastically: 'How about that for open doors! We had a church immediately.' She had a bigger surprise when she met one of her ex-Bible class students from Cambodia. He told her: 'While I was running from the Communists, I prayed to the Jesus Christ of whom I had heard to help me.'

When Gene Hall arrived at the camp he was able to baptise 44 new Cambodian believers, and to teach many the way of salvation.

From the camp the Cambodians went out to join American society, but before they could do so, someone had to agree to be responsible for their welfare. Churches and families helped, taking in individuals or families, clothing and feeding them and finding them a job. One church, at Salem in Oregon, sponsored 68 Cambodians, who became a Cambodian church within a church. They were led by Joe Kong Sarom and his wife Molyse, both new believers.

Some Cambodian children went to Holland shortly before Cambodia fell to the Communists, and they were taken in by two older Christian families. Four girls stayed with one couple, and two boys and a little girl with another family. But a Dutch board of adoption ruled the couples too old to adopt, and the children were taken from their new homes. One group was placed with a Roman Catholic family, and the other group was sent to a Hindu family. The children all had a Christian faith, and it was hard for them to leave their foster parents.

In America 20 sick children had been placed in Christian homes, but a doctor protested that World Vision should not be allowed to discriminate against non-Christians. He took the matter to court, and for a year the children became the subject of controversy, their new security placed in jeopardy. The court ruled against World Vision at first, but after a year the children, who had suffered so much upheaval in their short lives, were allowed to remain in their homes permanently. It was an answer to prayer.

The Church of Cambodia lived on in the lives of these small children, and in the lives of the refugees in many lands. During the first 18 months after the takeover, Jean Ellison, at Surin in Thailand, led 1,100 people to accept Christ. They held short-term Bible schools, and several hundred were baptised. Many told how much the love of the Christians had meant to them.

One refugee, Hong Sun Huor, filled with anxiety and despair when he reached Thailand, said: 'An hour after I entered the camp I saw a foreigner giving out relief supplies. He hurried over when he heard that I had just arrived. Putting his arms around me, he told me how glad he was that I had made it safely over. Tears came to my eyes. I just couldn't fathom why a white man would love me enough to be concerned about what had happened to me.

'That day he taught about God's love. Then he gave me a Cambodian New Testament. I took it to my quarters and read it avidly day after day, weighing carefully everything I read. My mind was still full of doubts. One day I realised that I was lost, separated from God. After a month and a half I invited the Lord into my heart, and He changed my life dramatically. Before I was restless; now I became calm. Before my heart was wicked and hateful; now I loved people as I would my own brother. Before I thought that I could depend on myself (until the labours of ten years were swept away); now I wanted to follow God's leading.'

Man's inhumanity to man could be seen clearly in Cambodia. Corpses lined every route to freedom, and those who fled faced booby traps, mines, patrolling guards and many ugly reminders of what their fate would be if they were caught. Skeletons whitened in the sun, swollen bodies of men, women and children unburied were commonplace in parts of Cambodia. Still, many chose to escape and face death rather than live in a 'big concentration camp'. Under cover of the forests, they headed for Thailand and freedom.

Once Chhirc said: 'Pray for Cambodia, and pray that the powers of darkness will be removed.' That prayer was needed more than ever in the land of death.

14 Through the Darkness

Thirty years before Cambodia was lost to the Khmer Rouge, in a peaceful village near Battambang a Christian farmer gathered his family together and told them: 'There is great trouble ahead for my beloved country. You must keep faith in the Lord, no matter what terrible things happen to you.' Six years before Cambodia fell he died, and never saw the fulfilment of his prophecy.

His son, Sousten, was a captain in the Army defending Phnom Penh when the order was given to lay down arms. He tried to get home to change his Army uniform, but he never made it. Khmer Rouge soldiers told him to remove his shirt, insignia and shoes, and tied his hands behind his back, saying: 'Friend, we don't trust you.' He was taken to a prison where about 4,000 officers were being held.

Later that same afternoon trucks arrived and took them to an 'indoctrination session'. Sousten found he was being driven south with a group of about 1,000, but soon the trucks were halted. The prisoners were ordered out and told to arrange themselves in a long line. Armed soldiers then lined up behind the officers, and the order was given to fire.

The bullet meant for Sousten ricocheted over his shoulder, but the shock made him fall to the ground in a dead faint. When the bodies were checked and he was found to be breathing, he was beaten mercilessly with gnarled, spiney clubs and left for dead.

Ten hours later he recovered consciousness. Dead bodies surrounded him. He was the sole survivor.

Refugees straggled past on the nearby road, but no one dared respond to his cry for help. Then, at dawn, a

Chinese boy came over to him, cut his ropes and whispered: 'Meet me up ahead. It isn't safe for me here.' Despite his pain, and the blood he was coughing up, Sousten managed to reach the place the Chinese boy had indicated. The boy was waiting there with his family, and Sousten hobbled along the road with them until they reached a small village. Exhausted, he told them to go on without him, but the kindly Chinese family refused.

That night Sousten tossed and turned in pain under the tree where he slept. He cried out to the Lord to help him find some medicine for the relief of the unbearable pain in his chest, and as he slept he dreamt. 'The Lord was standing beside me, and I heard a voice say: "You will not die, but will live to help your countrymen." Again the voice spoke: "Peel some bark from the tree under which you are lying, and then brew it." '

Sousten awoke in the early dawn, and because of the vividness of the dream he peeled off the bark of the tree and made a brew — then blacked out for hours. When they restarted their journey to Kampot he was able to walk normally, and completed the seven days with fresh energy.

After reaching Kampot the little group were moved 125 miles away to another area, where they worked from dawn till eleven at night, with two scanty meals of rice. Seven months later Sousten was moved again, separated from his Chinese friends and sent to work in a group at Kompong Thom, near Thailand.

There Sousten was betrayed by another Cambodian and interrogated by five soldiers. He did not know why he was not killed there and then, but instead one of the guards was told: 'We will be back in three days to execute him.' The Red Guard was sorry for Sousten, and at the risk of his own life told him: 'They are coming to get you. Your only chance is to escape. Here is a knife and a supply of rice.' Sousten knew the man was risking his own life in helping him, and it seemed another miracle.

That night he headed east for Thailand, knowing it would take him many tense, dangerous days to reach the border.

On the way he acquired seven companions who had also found life unbearable under the Khmer Rouge regime. Sousten prayed out loud as he travelled, which annoyed some of them; so five decided to go it alone. They had not gone far when enemy soldiers caught them, and they were bound and led away.

The remaining three men were warned by the Lord to go another way, and found the only possible route. At dusk Sousten crept back through the undergrowth to see what had happened to his former companions. He watched in horror at the enemy camp site as the captives were thrown, one by one, into the fire. There was nothing he could do; he thanked the Lord that he had escaped death once again.

Sousten and his two companions, an Army medic and a professor, travelled together for the next four days. But then they came to a clearing, and the professor decided to skirt it where the going was easier, rather than continue hacking through the undergrowth. He ignored the pleadings of the other two, but it was only moments before he was captured, and soon afterwards Sousten and Jeum saw Khmer Rouge soldiers heading towards their hiding place. The professor had obviously given them away. They ran hard, and although they saw soldiers chasing them, deep forest soon hid them from view.

For two days they journeyed on in the forest, but on the third day they reached the outskirts of a village and were forced to hide in long clumps of grass. Groups of villagers passed their hiding place, and children climbed trees overhead, while soldiers walked just two metres away—yet they were not seen. That night Jeum gave his life to Christ. He had seen many miracles on his road to freedom.

Fever-racked with malaria and swollen with malnutrition from living on what they could scrounge from the forest, the two men crossed the border in June, 1976. Sousten had lived to tell others of his faith and miraculous preservation, but the prophecy of his father had been horribly fulfilled.

*   *   *

The world knew little of the remaking of Cambodia. No news filtered out of the tightly-sealed country. But refugees told the story in their emaciated bodies, their bitter faces and in their words . . .

'They gave us three days to evacuate Pailin. At first the people just wondered, for they had not tasted the powerful medicine (ruthless methods) of the Khmer Rouge. Then the people began to leave, fleeing along the route mapped out, driven before the Khmer Rouge, who were beginning to put their plans into effect. There were no jails or chains, just the muzzles of guns prodding us along. The road from Pailin to Battambang on either side was strewn with rotting corpses, filling the air with their stench. There was no way of knowing why or when these people were killed.'

*   *   *

'As we have a large family, we were unable to bring any food or supplies. It was all we could do to save the children; so we didn't bring anything else. Lacking food, we begged from the villagers, and they gave us small amounts, enough to make some rice gruel for the children. We also foraged from the gardens of people who had run off. From them we got enough only to feed ourselves.

'Later the Khmer Rouge divided us into groups of ten families, and for each group issued a ration of two bags of unhusked rice, supposedly for one week's food supply. These rations were given out irregularly . . .

'From then on people began dying of starvation, as many had neither gold nor wrist watches to trade for rice. Later those who had had gold or wrist watches found themselves without assets, and they were then in the same boat as everyone else. People died wholesale in a steady stream of malnutrition, disease and starvation. In some families all the children died; in others the wife or husband died; still others suffered the loss of both parents, leaving only the small children to fend for themselves.

'Others, unable to stand such conditions any longer, spoke out against what is called the "organisation". They were taken out and clubbed to death, as if they were animals — and not buried, but tossed to the side of the roads as a warning to others who might be tempted to follow their rebellious example.'

*   *   *

'My two little ones were as thin as two sticks,' recounted Loeung Savin. 'We had no milk for them; they were only skin and bones. My wife could no longer feed the baby, as her own milk supply stopped. Their little bodies alternately swelled and shrank from lack of essential vitamins. I lost all hope that they would live, because of their physical condition. That night my wife and I prayed constantly, and they began to improve. I knew that this was the Lord's answer to our prayers.

'I tried to pray even more, telling the Lord with tears that I could no longer live with these people because they were so indescribably vicious. They considered us villagers the "enemy". They permit no religion . . . There is only planting and hoeing potatoes, corn and rice from sun-up till sun-down, unless we fall in our traces.

'I prayed continually that somehow the Lord would open up a way for me to lead my family out from under the Communist yoke. But week by week I was thwarted in my efforts, hearing constantly of those who had tried to escape and had been shot, their bodies tossed aside, because they had tried to reach Thailand.

'On November 10th, 1975 I decided to leave my family and flee by night. I had little hope of surviving. I decided to find a way out for my family even if I died in the attempt. At least I would have tried, and I committed my adventure into the Lord's hands. In exactly one week I made it to Thailand. I had walked through forests, over mountains and under overhanging rocks, not daring to go into the fields and valleys lest they see me. Occasionally I had to slither and crawl across roads. At last I crossed the border into Thailand on the evening of the seventh day at about 5 pm, about 300 yards from a group of Khmer Rouge on my left . . . We could see the smoke of their rice pots, and later in the evening we heard their voices as they talked together in the forest.

'Arriving at Klong Yai refugee camp, I reached an all-time low of discouragement, for my hopes of rescuing my family were dashed. I was so overcome with difficulties that I lay down and cried, with such a tightening of my chest that I felt it would burst, just thinking of my wife and children, and all my Cambodian compatriots. We had heard reports that the soldiers who had escaped to Thailand were forming into groups to free Cambodia. It was completely false information. I lived every day in hopelessness.

'I tried to read the Bible and pray constantly, but in a short time I came down with severe malaria, and I had to be given blood transfusions. It took a long time to recover. Though still not completely well, I escaped from the refugee camp back to Cambodia, and in five days and nights made it back to my family. I didn't dare approach the village, but stayed in the forest by the mountainside until I was able to slip in to meet my family at night. It took two days to get our family together, as the Communists had taken my nephews to work on a dam project.

'When we were finally all together, we left at 8 pm. There were 15 of us, including my sister, her children and her daughter-in-law. That night we marched clear through till daylight, because we had to be well into the forest to be hidden from them.

'Each day before we started out we always prayed together as a family. The nights were terribly cold, sleeping as we were on the ground under the trees. Sometimes we were without water and had to pan-fry the rice kernels by night underground, so that they wouldn't see the smoke. After five days our food gave out. On the sixth, seventh and eighth days we were close to the gardens of former

Pailin folk and near the mountains, so that, hiding our family in the forest, we men were able to pull up potatoes by the roots to boil and eat.

'On the eighth evening we made it into Thailand. Praise the Lord! He was with us all the way, so that we were safe and did not run into "them", as others did, whom they met and shot, piling their bodies one on top of the other, old and young alike. God indeed gave me the courage and fortitude to bring my family out.

'Two of my nephews-in-law who came with us saw the wonderful ways the Lord answered prayer, and they repented and gave themselves to Christ without my knowing about it until later. They went to the refugee chapel the day after our arrival, and accepted Christ. I really thank the Lord. I find that I am at an all-time high of faith in the Lord.'

* * *

The fact that there were still Christians coming out of Cambodia was proof enough that there were others left behind. They were dispersed throughout the country, effectively cut off from each other, unable to meet together, yet the Lord was preserving them. Wherever the Christians were, they had taken the Gospel message with them, and their lives stood as a witness to the God who promised never to leave or forsake them. The holocaust of destruction could not destroy the Christian Church of Cambodia. The powers of evil and hell could cause havoc, but 'where there is a desperate people, there is a yet more powerful God'.

* * *

A young Chinese teenager who had often visited the youth centre in Phnom Penh arrived in Thailand. He had been separated from his family and sent to work near the border. He said: 'I worked in the fields, where I lived with about 5,000 others. I got up every morning at 4 am to cook rice, which the soldiers gave along with salt. Only 20 soldiers were needed to guard so many people. Food, which was desperately needed, was gained by selling possessions. Dogs were eaten to stave off hunger pains . . . Work was seven days a week.

'In this group there were about ten Christians, all Chinese. There were some Bibles. About five people met together for prayer. We had no fear of death, even though some were taken away and shot, and many were scared.'

Cambodia had become a land of fear, darkness and hate. Grass grew in the boulevards of Phnom Penh and shops stood as though derelict, with open shutters. No children played on the streets. It was said that when Prince Sihanouk returned to his land and saw the desolation of Phnom Penh, he wept.

People toiled in the fields, away from the towns. Factories and dams were built in remote places. Singing was forbidden, drinking and dancing despised, and the people were educated to chant at regular intervals revolutionary slogans like 'Cambodia is building the only true Communism'. Children were spies for the new Cambodia, and had to report even their parents to the soldiers.

Stories carried out by the fleeing Cambodians were very different from the reports of Radio Phnom Penh, which proclaimed: 'The scenery is fresh, the plants are fresh, life is fresh and people are smiling.' Those escaping to Thailand told of continued killing and inhuman conditions. One refugee said: 'I met the pastor from Battambang with his children, and although he was distraught we were able to pray together.'

The church at Battambang was destroyed, as was the beautiful TaKhmau Bible school building. All 'reactionary religion' was punishable by death. For the Cambodian Communists there were no lesser penalties; anything not in line with revolutionary thought—including speaking a foreign language—could lead to death.

Temples and churches were used as ammunition depots.

The Khmer Rouge wanted no reminders of the past to taint their 'glorious and wonderful' revolution. Many spoke of piles of literature stacked in the streets of towns and burnt, and many arriving in Thailand had not seen any Cambodian literature at all for over a year. Yet some had managed to keep their Bibles.

One Christian who escaped described vividly the suffering of the people and the faith that remained. 'The Khmer population does not cease to die of hunger and illness', he said. 'All Christians suffer. One of my friends is a remarkable Christian; he does not cease to give thanks to God. He prays each day. Unfortunately, he has still not been able to flee. But I am sure that God will give him the opportunity, because he never ceases to praise God each day, and I myself pray for him.'

Wounded in the foot, this young man had survived the gruelling journey through dense forest to tell of a vibrant, radiant faith that had overcome trials and disaster. The truth of God's love was a match for the paralysis of hate that had engulfed Cambodia.

Inside Cambodia the Word of God could still be heard—beamed in on Medium Wave from Manila. The broadcasts began in June, 1975, as an act of faith, because no one knew whether they would have any listeners. Stories from refugees soon made it clear that they did. One man spoke of using an old car battery to power his radio so that he could tune in.

One Cambodian diplomat who had fled his country wrote: 'I have a hard time hearing you. Could you speak up into the microphone? Could you send me a book about God, because I want to be one of those whom He loves like He loves you? . . . In closing, may Jesus Christ grant His blessing and uphold you as you work at the Radio Voice of Love, that you may have peace.'

Lim Chheong and Keam Ny Sumido were involved with Paul and Eunice Ellison, two C&MA missionaries, in producing the programmes. They were helped later by a young Cambodian girl called Samoeurn, who reached

Manila by boat from Cambodia because she wanted 'a new life away from the violence'. When Keam Ny visited her she gave her life to Christ and began to train for radio work.

In one of the refugee camps an escaped Khmer Rouge soldier gave his life to Christ after listening to radio broadcasts. A refugee from among the hostile Cham people heard and believed inside Cambodia before his escape. God was showing that the Gospel could penetrate any barrier. Turmoil and change would not blunt the impact of the Holy Spirit on the lives of the Cambodian people. Greater things could be expected in Cambodia, and prayer would bring them to pass.

Thousands of Cambodians and Chinese made their way to South Vietnam, where one Cambodian missionary remained preaching and ministering to a growing congregation. He wrote to Lim Chheong: 'Daily we receive spiritual food through the Radio Voice of Love that you broadcast, and so do our church people. We shall not forget to pray for you, that the Lord will give you health at all times so that you may become the central pillar in the spread of the Good News, which is pleasing to our Lord Jesus Christ. Amen; please pray for us that we might have strength and good health to serve in Vietnam in order to care for the Lord's lambs and give them daily food in sufficient supply. They are most hungry and thirsty now for spiritual nourishment. We tune in our radios every day for this. Thank the Lord.'

A few foreigners, meanwhile, were allowed into Cambodia on guided tours. They were watched closely and not allowed to go out alone into the country. One diplomat said: 'I saw thousands working, like a people at war, planting rice. The towns of Cambodia were ghost-like, and it was hard to imagine that once they had been thriving, bustling places.' The refugees told their own stories of what it was like to live in Cambodia under the Angka Loeu — the 'Organisation on High'.

On May 5th 1977 a Christian who had once been a student at the TaKhmau Bible school crossed into Thailand

with some members of the resistance movement. The
border was by this time very hazardous, as four miles of
forest had been cleared and mined to prevent people
escaping. In the camps he witnessed to his love for the
Lord, two years after the fall of Cambodia.

In desperate situations men draw near to God as they
realise how little they can do to help themselves. One
refugee told how he had been converted after the Communist takeover. 'I planted rice with a man who was a
Christian', he said, 'and he told me how I too could
become a Christian.'

Miracles were still happening in Cambodia, and the
Lord was revealing Himself in the lives of the Christians
there.

15 The Living Stones

Sawat was a young Christian of 22 when he died in a refugee camp. He had fallen sick, his only medicine had been Multivite and iron tablets, and a missionary found him lying in a long shed. On the Thursday he died . . .

'We got him to hospital, but no one wanted the body. Then the camp chief arrived in his Land Rover and took us to a building where we had to wait two hours for a coffin. We then went to the cemetery, where he was buried. It was a lovely spot.' As the Christians stood around the grave in the blazing sun, Saroeng whispered, 'He applied for a third country, and Jesus has taken him!'

The war in South-East Asia was to many a past event, and the flotsam of war was just the unfortunate aftermath. Some countries, like America and France, welcomed refugees, but others had little concern for 'someone else's problem.' For Christians the outcast is a neighbour, to be cared for. Jesus was once a refugee.

One of those visiting the camp close to the border at Aranyaprathet was Don Cormack. Though he went there every day, it was a while before he noticed the man in the camp clinic. The wooden building on stilts was constantly occupied and it was easy to miss people. But one day he saw the man with his thin wasted body, his swollen stomach disfigured by a long scar. Don could have wept at the state of him—feet caked with mud, hair thick and matted, a filthy cloth around him. Nobody knew him, and he was alone.

Don bent down and spoke to him in Cambodian, but his eyes were glazed and he made no reply. The sign hanging on his bed read 'Sopat'. Don went to find the doctor to see what could be done. 'Hopeless', said the doctor. 'Full of cancer, but do what you like for him.' Don returned to Sopat's bedside, his heart aching at the situation. This time Sopat turned and looked at him, and wept soundlessly as Don bent and washed his face, and gave him a drink. After fetching him a new sarong Don went home.

Back at his house, Don felt weighed down with sorrow and poured it out to the One who cares. Even in his own personal agony he knew how much God loved this man. He had seen other Cambodians die, but Sopat's awful aloneness had struck him and he could not get him out of his mind.

On returning to the clinic with the washed sarong he talked with the man about his home and family. Cleaning him up took a long time, and as Don was finishing Sopat surprised him with a question, 'How can I know what will happen to me after death?'

It was a joy to talk to him about Jesus and the living God. Sopat was excited. 'I believe it, yes I believe it. I believe in Jesus—He is the Truth.' Don went to find Pol Chhorn, a Christian who had just escaped to Thailand after living in the forests of Cambodia for two years. When they returned Sopat whispered, 'Has he come to tell me more about Jesus?' Pol Chhorn smiled, and with tender love told him the moving story of the dying thief on the cross who was promised he would be with Jesus in paradise. As Sopat listened the words brought balm and healing, driving away his fear and uncertainty and leaving him full of peace.

Every day the Cambodian Christians came and cared for him, sharing all they had with him. At the end Don and the others were with him, and they felt the presence of the Lord as his breathing became shallower and then finally stopped. His face had a deep serenity and they knew he had gone to be with Jesus in paradise. Six of the Christians, including Pol Chhorn, were given permission to go to the graveside.

The grave was in the place for the vagrants and very

poor, yet Chhorn's voice rang out clear and strong, 'Victory is complete! Where, death, is your victory?' Sopat was no longer an unwanted person, but a member of that great number of the Lord's people who would always be with Him.

Only a few days later Don met two men who had once been friends of Sopat. He went up and told them about Sopat's faith, and his death. They were moved to tears, and one said, 'It is truly amazing. He was such a wicked and feared thief in Cambodia.'

The new fellowships in the refugee camps were fluctuating constantly, as people moved on to a new life in their 'third country'. As time dragged on, one refugee puzzled and grappled with his own question, and decided at last to draft a letter to a missionary:

'Since my immigration to Thailand I have participated in every Christian meeting led by the Rev. John Ellison. I have a great deal of free time to read the New Testament and other books of the Bible. I have learned several verses by heart. However, I feel guilty because I am living at the camp and not working for my keep. I believe this to be very bad, for God said to man: "It is by hard work alone that you shall earn your food, every day of your life. It is by your own sweat that you shall eat your bread."

'But I feel that God has given me precious opportunity to learn and study the Bible. In the camp I often ask myself, "Who am I?" My reply sometimes is, "I am a Christian, and my one task in life is to study the Bible." But sometimes I answer that I am a refugee, separated from my parents and country, and living in a camp without earning my keep. My life is absurd, has no meaning, and I am nothing but an idle worker. I have many sins . . . I beg you to justify the above answers if you will. And so that God will pardon me and save me . . . I have decided to make my sacrifice before God.'

In a refugee camp people become reliant on others for their food, and even their passport to freedom. Waiting brings despair, and many read the Bible and study it as a way of escape from their often overcrowded, noisy surroundings.

A new camp was erected to replace the one where Sawat died, but the benefits of the improved conditions were lost as more and more people escaped from the 'liberated' countries. Within the camps there was both sorrow and joy as families lived under their hastily-erected shelters.

One day a crowd gathered at a shelter when a man led three small children in. He explained: 'We were separated from my wife in the forest, on our trek across the border.' All of them stood there in rags. John and Jean Ellison said: 'Our hearts were once more wrenched by the cruel suffering of so many innocent ones.'

The man was Jang Beung, who had been a soldier when Cambodia fell. He lived with his family 50 miles from the Thai border. He had thought he would be safe if he surrendered his arms — after all, he told himself, 'I am just an ordinary soldier.' This confidence was quickly shaken as a cattle dealer told him what had happened to a group of soldiers who were taken to Angkor Wat, ostensibly for a Buddhist ceremony. They were forced to dig their own graves before being struck down with hoes and dumped in.

So Jang Beung decided to escape, with a group of about 50 others. But after a day's trek through the forest half of the group were suddenly attacked by Khmer Rouge soldiers. A baby was killed when its mother stumbled and fell, everybody scattered and Jang Beung lost his eldest son in the confusion. With food gone they continued their journey for another day, but by nightfall Jang Beung's wife, Cheun Teng, fell ill with a violent fever and became so dizzy that she could walk no further. Her husband left a hammock and a small bundle of clothes, deciding to carry on with the children to Thailand and come back for her. He arrived safely in Thailand, but when he went back for his wife all he found was their few possessions, and he thought the Communists had got her. He returned in sorrow to the refugee camp.

Cheun Teng, however, had not been captured. The

night her husband and children left her she had slept very little, tossing and turning and feeling very thirsty. She struggled to reach water nearby, and drank, but was then unable to find her way back to the hammock. For eight days her only bed was the ground, and she had no food, but each day she forced herself to travel a little further. She said: 'I had no fear as I walked along, because I felt the presence of several people walking just ahead of me, leading the way.'

After four days of walking her feet were so badly swollen that she could hardly hobble. Every movement was agony. When her strength gave out and she lay exhausted she fell asleep. 'I dreamt that someone gave me a lemon drink, and when I awoke I felt I could go on.'

On the eighth day she reached a small shelter in a potato patch, her legs so swollen and lacerated by thorns that she could go no further. Four days later she was found—more dead than alive—by the owner and his wife, who came to work in the garden, and they took her home and cared for her.

Without knowing, she had arrived in Thailand.

She stayed there seven days, and was then taken in an oxcart to meet her husband. He met her halfway, overjoyed to find that the wife he had thought dead was alive—and safe. Those who saw her in her weakened, starved condition could hardly believe she had made the dangerous journey to Thailand unguided and alone. It did not seem possible.

Ten days later both Jang Beung and Cheun Teng gave their lives to Christ. They recognised, as did many, that only the Lord and his guiding angels had shown her the way. To complete their happiness the missing oldest son also made it to Thailand with another group, and the whole family was reunited.

*   *   *

Thousands of refugees still sit helplessly in Thailand. By 1977 agricultural schemes were introduced in some camps, and some farming was allowed. C&MA began a project to enable refugees to sew and sell their handicrafts abroad, and World Vision has provided schooling for about 5,000 children. Many organisations help to make life easier.

For a while at least, refugees are able to go on to other lands, but there is little hope of everyone being allowed to leave for a 'third country'. The end of 1977 saw 80,000 refugees still in Thailand, about 11,000 of them Cambodians, and more keep pouring in. Refugee boats appear regularly on the shores of Thailand; passengers in these small fishing vessels are often refused permission to land and are confined to the cramped conditions on board for many months. Many of the boats have been lost at sea, but others keep on coming.

The long wait for clearance to leave is suffered by refugees not only in Thailand but also in Vietnam, where many are still stranded, hoping to be able to start again in America, France or elsewhere.

One woman waited 20 months to leave Ho Chi Minh City. Her parents had been part of the early Evangelical Church in Cambodia after her father, an immoral, dissolute Frenchman, was led to the Lord by a Cambodian. He was married to a Cambodian who had despaired of changing his ways, but when he became a Christian she was so impressed with the difference in his life that she prayed: 'Lord, if you are real, show yourself to me.' Immediately she had a vision of Christ standing before her, dressed in the most beautiful robes she had ever seen — and from that moment she believed.

Nellie was this couple's only daughter. A firm Christian, she was a great friend of Princess Norodom Rasmi Sobhana, who once said to her: 'Every time I think of you, I think of your God.'

Nellie grew up in Cambodia, and she never intended to leave. When the Communists stormed into Phnom Penh she took refuge in the French embassy, along with Chhirc Taing and Minh Thien Voan. But on April 21st the Khmer Rouge demanded that all Cambodians should leave the protection of the embassy. She saw Chhirc and Minh Thien Voan bundled on to a lorry and tried to get on to the same truck, but a guard looked at a list in his hand and said: 'You are a nobody. You can go.' The truck drove away, and she was left standing outside the embassy. It was the last she saw of Chhirc and Minh Thien Voan.

Nellie could have stayed in the safety of the embassy, for she had a French passport, but she chose to go and look for her niece Kanya and servant Sombat, whom she found, by a miracle, among the crowds of people streaming out of the city. They decided to make their way to Thailand. 'We walked among the dead and found the roads very slow, as no one could travel far', she said. 'It was impossible to get through that way, as the people were watched by silent soldiers.'

Realising that the three of them had little hope of reaching Thailand on their own, they found a man who promised to help a group of 20 of them reach freedom by way of South Vietnam. Only the three of them were Christians. Living off roots and wild fruit, they made the gruelling journey through the forests, and eventually arrived in South Vietnam. The rest of their group went off without paying the guide, but the three Christians, although they had no money, did not want to avoid paying. As they were walking along they saw a coin in the dust at their feet. It was gold! The guide, who had been sceptical of their faith during the journey, was surprised and delighted when they presented it to him. 'God is real,' Nellie told him.

But having reached South Vietnam, they found it was not easy to leave. Nellie was determined not to leave her old servant and niece, although she had a French passport to freedom. For 20 months she worked to get papers for them and lived and worshipped with the Vietnamese Christians, sharing their sorrows and joys. Her faith and trust were rewarded, and in April 1977 she arrived in France with her companions, to join the small group of Cambodian believers worshipping in Paris.

Working among the Cambodians there were Jean Jacques

and Marie Piaget, a couple who had served in Cambodia and had a ministry to the refugees scattered throughout France.

The immigrants were haunted by frustration, bitterness and their own private agonies. Most had suffered the loss of loved ones. Many had first heard the Gospel in Thailand, land of temples and idols, but in France another god reigned — materialism. Sometimes television became an object of worship: many who had never seen it before could hardly resist it. The enemy now was of a different, more subtle kind. Jean Jacques and his family did what they could to soften the 'culture shock', helping refugees in practical ways and directing them to French churches.

Half the Cambodians in France lived near Paris, but those 'living stones' scattered throughout the country often had little fellowship and few friends. Leaders were scarce; only Ung Davy was full time. For these people a Cambodian Retreat in the beautiful mountains close to Switzerland was of special value, and very moving. Here they shared the past and their hopes for the future, their testimonies marked by faith in the face of danger. Many could understand what it meant to have lost all touch with loved ones for the rest of their lives, because it had also happened to them.

But loneliness haunts most who come to France. It is devastating suddenly to be the only one.

Ung Davy grew up in Phnom Penh with his uncle and aunt, became a Christian and decided to train to serve the Lord. The Cambodian Church asked him to go to France to study, and he was accepted by Nogent Bible Institute, near Paris. When Phnom Penh fell his heart ached as he thought of his family and friends, and he sought guidance for the future.

He finished his college course, but felt inadequate for the task of reaching the many thousands of Cambodian refugees in France, and so he decided to cement his training and also improve his English by studying at the Abbey Missionary School of English. There he met Ruth, a Swiss girl, whom he married in November 1977. After their marriage they committed themselves to the work of reaching refugees in France and building up the scattered Cambodian church there.

Their small apartment in Paris was a place where many came and talked of their problems and difficulties. During their courtship Ruth had written to Davy the beautiful words of her namesake: 'Entreat me not to leave you or return from following you; for where you go I will go, and where you lodge I will lodge; your people shall be my people and your God my God; where you die I will die, and there will I be buried. May the Lord do so to me and more also if even death parts me from you.'

Davy and Ruth worked hard in Paris and built up the Church there. Davy visited the hostels, welcoming new refugees to France and linking them to fellowships in other parts of the country, where they were sent. On visits to England he spoke with conviction of his concern for the people of his country. He knew the suffering, loneliness and frustrations of refugees from his own experience. 'I am a refugee, but in one sense we are all refugees', he would often say.

Kim Vé, a Christian mother whose two sons were left behind in Cambodia, is part of the fellowship in Paris. She said: 'We know the love of God joins us together as brothers and sisters with those who are believers throughout the world.' Her husband, Chay Son, was converted in Paris, but she herself first believed in Phnom Penh. She did not know what had happened to her two sons, who were living with her grandmother when Phnom Penh fell, while she was away with her husband and two other children.

During a trip to Paris we visited Kim Vé and Chay Son and showed them the pictures which Chhirc and others had given us. They gave a shout of joy when they saw the photo of a Sunday school class in Phnom Penh, because in the class sat their two boys! They had no other photo of them.

There must still today be many children in Cambodia separated from or deprived of their Christian parents. We must pray they will remember that where there is hatred,

Jesus taught love. The Cambodian Church has been built on prayer and is kept alive by prayer, for God has promised to answer the prayers of faith. It must be a very precious Church to God, for it has withstood much suffering and been tested in the fires of evil.

In July 1978 Davy and Ruth were killed in a car crash, along with the youngest daughter of Chay Son and Kim Vé. The eldest daughter, Sophaline, and Ruth's mother survived, although they were critically ill for a long time. In the dead girl's Bible were written the words: 'I have given my heart to Jesus.'

Just three months before his death, Davy had spoken at a *Cambodia for Christ* meeting in London on the theme of suffering and glory. The people of Cambodia all seem to be touched by the agonies being suffered behind the closed frontier. The Church is certainly not immune in other lands. But Chay Son and Kim Vé remain faithful to the Lord, and Sophaline is a shining example of Christian faith.

These Christians have been through the fires of experience and have remained strong. On the night Davy and Ruth died, Arun, a young Cambodian Christian, heard God call him to train at Bible school; and Try Seng Ly, a pastor's son who went to the same college as Davy, preaches in Paris with enthusiasm and is praying about his future. Norman and Marie Ens are also going to work in France as the Church in Paris seeks guidance. The seeds of a powerful Cambodian Church in France are sown.

Another man from the Paris fellowship had seen his wife killed in Phnom Penh. With his three small children he had walked many miles to Ho Chi Minh City, through the forest and over tracks and roads, finally reaching Thailand by sea.

Keat, the young Cambodian sailor who gave his life to the Lord during the storm, also worships in Paris. Two of his brothers escaped to Thailand—but not his favourite sister, who is still in Cambodia.

The gay city of Paris only accentuates the losses of these

Cambodians, who work to establish roots in France, knowing they can never go home.

*   *   *

In America, too, Cambodian Christians suffered the shock that comes with a change of culture. The bewildering cities and rapid pace of life made many wonder if they were in the right place, and some were given direct reassurance.

Kuch Kong and family arrived in Oklahoma with some small children at the end of 1975, and were given an apartment. One night his wife San woke up, and the Lord spoke to her: 'I'm giving you a promise. Jeremiah 42, verses 9-12, as a promise to you and your family. It will be a pillar of hope for you to cling to in the future.'

Together Kuch Kong and San turned to the words from Jeremiah: 'Thus says the Lord the God of Israel, to whom you sent me to present your petitions before Him: If you will indeed stay in this land, then I will build you up and not tear you down, and I will plant you and not uproot you; for I shall relent concerning the calamity that I have inflicted on you. Do not be afraid of the King of Babylon, whom you are now fearing. Do not be afraid of him, declares the Lord, for I am with you to save you and deliver you from his hand. I will also show you compassion, so that he will have compassion on you and restore you to your own soil.'*

They began a course of study at *Christ for the Nations* College, and Kuch Kong began visiting Cambodians and sending out cassettes to those in need of fellowship.

Lim Chheong, Hannah and their three children stayed in the Philippines until their passports expired and they became stateless. They moved to the USA, and in California continued the same ministry, with Paul and Eunice Ellison, of producing radio programmes for beaming into Cambodia. They began to invite others into their home to share

*Jeremiah 42.9-12 (American Standard Version).

the Gospel, and Lim Chheong also began producing teaching cassettes to send to lonely Cambodian believers.

It was never easy for the Cambodian exiles, but their faith remained firm in suffering. Joe Kong Sarom, the young leader at Salem Church in Oregon, saw the Cambodian fellowship there growing. His wife, Molyse, opened their home to whoever came to the door, and shared all she had. But one day she fell seriously ill and was rushed into hospital to have a lung operation. When she recovered consciousness she sang the chorus, 'I have decided to follow Jesus', then slipped into a coma, and died three days later.

Joe was left without a wife, and with five small children to bring up. He and his wife had been Christians only a year, and yet he wrote: 'As one of God's children I must live, walk and stand by faith. Faith pleases God more than anything else. I am sure that Jesus hears every cry of my heart. Jesus wants me to know that He is the same as He always has been. He is on His throne. He wants me to know that the Heavenly Father knows what He is doing. What He is doing is best for Molyse, my children and myself. He is a perfect God. He makes no mistakes.'

A year later we learned that the Lord had given Joe a new partner.

God is giving new life to others among the Cambodian people; so the Church of Cambodia will not die. God never makes a mistake. The Church in Cambodia was a living, vibrant Church in the face of tragedy and death—a shining example of the power of the Holy Spirit in adverse circumstances. The new Cambodian Church born out of darkness has that same vitality and faith.

Over a year after the Khmer Rouge took Phnom Penh, Bophana, Chhirc's wife, received two things on the same day: a photograph of Chhirc sent from Australia, and a letter from him, written before he was taken from the French embassy by the Communists. The letter had been brought out of Cambodia by one of the foreigners permitted to leave; it had gone to Thailand, then to France, eventually reaching Bophana in Scotland, where she was living with her little girl. In the letter Chhirc asks the Christians of Europe and elsewhere not to forget to pray for Cambodia, and sends his love to them.

*   *   *

The fall of Phnom Penh is now history. Few can visit Cambodia today, but all can pray. In Thailand, in 1977, the first Cambodian Church building was completed — Klong Yai Baptist Church, with 250 Cambodians as members. In America there were five Cambodian churches, and in other countries there are groups and churches forming. *Cambodia for Christ,* which was formed in 1973, continues to encourage people to become concerned and above all to pray for the people of Cambodia. One day some of us may not have a home, and we may be stateless. As Christians we cannot wait; we must care. The Cambodian people need us to be their brothers and sisters. They need a new family.

From New Zealand we received the following letter from a Cambodian, Ung BunLeng:

'I used to hate the Gospel; to me, it was only a product of western culture, an opiate for the poor and stricken. I remember one of my relatives who attended the Gospel singing rally led by Dr Mooneyham (I refused to go because I knew it was those funny Christians again!). He came back visibly moved and started asking me, Why do those "white men" still naïvely believe in God? (As you could guess, "white men" are closely linked with progress and knowledge.)

'I understood why two years later, when one night I decided to make it clear once and for all whether the Gospel works or not. I asked Jesus to come into my heart and change me. At that moment I knew the joy of the Spirit flooding deep down in me. I would have shouted if I knew what to shout; I would have danced if I had known

King David did that. I fully understood God's love when four days later I received the Spirit of God.'

Ung BunLeng shared a flat with other Cambodians, and he witnessed to them about his new life in Christ, and how hatred could be overcome by the love of God.

The key to any Christian's life is prayer. Where prayer is raised up there is a God who listens and answers, and the impossible can happen. Inside Cambodia there is awful darkness, but where one Christian remains, a light shines on. The boundaries of Cambodia contain a Church which must not be forgotten.

'For the Lamb in the midst of the throne will be their shepherd, and he will guide them to the springs of living water; and God will wipe away every tear from their eyes.'

A prayer for the Cambodians, adapted from Psalm 119:

Your word is a lamp to the Cambodians' feet
and a light to their path;
There are those who have sworn an oath and confirmed it,
to obscure your righteous ordinances.
The Cambodians are sorely afflicted:
give them life, O Lord, according to your word.
Accept their offerings of praise, O Lord,
and teach them your ordinances.
They hold their lives in their hands continually,
but let them not forget your law.
The wicked have laid a snare for them,
but may the Cambodians not forget your law.
Yea, may it be the joy of their hearts.
May they incline their hearts to perform your statutes
for ever, to the end.